THE QUIET
HEROES

By the same author

Masters Next to God
They Sank the Red Dragon
The Fighting Tramps
The Grey Widow Maker
Blood and Bushido
SOS – Men Against the Sea
Salvo!
Attack and Sink
Dönitz and the Wolf Packs
Return of the Coffin Ships
Beware Raiders!
The Road to Russia

THE QUIET HEROES

BRITISH MERCHANT SEAMEN AT WAR

by

BERNARD EDWARDS

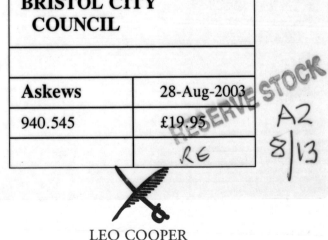

LEO COOPER

First published in Great Britain in 2003 by
LEO COOPER
an imprint of Pen & Sword Books
47 Church Street,
Barnsley,
South Yorkshire,
S70 2AS

Copyright © 2003 by Bernard Edwards

ISBN 0 85052 911 5

A catalogue record for this book
is available from the British Library

Typeset in 11/13pt Sabon by
Phoenix Typesetting, Burley-in-Wharfedale, West Yorkshire

Printed in England by CPI UK

This book is dedicated to the men of Britain's merchant fleet
who gave their lives in the Second World War.

Unrecognised, you put us in your debt;
Unthanked, you enter or escape the grave;
Whether your land remember or forget
You saved the land, or died to try to save.

John Masefield, *For All Seafarers*

Contents

1

Prologue

Being an island with limited natural resources, Britain has always been largely dependent on her merchant shipping for her survival and prosperity. She cannot hope to exist for long without food for her population, oil for her transport, and raw materials for her manufacturing industries. This weakness was magnified tenfold during the Second World War, when Britain could never have been anything more than a transient bulwark of Western democracy without substantial aid from her dominions and the United States of America. Her merchant fleet was therefore her maritime jugular, stretched tight and often dangerously exposed. From the first hours of the outbreak of war, Britain's old naval adversary, Germany, took her sharpened knife to the pulsating vein.

The men of Britain's Merchant Navy, although unarmed civilians going about their normal business, were the first to be involved in the war against Nazi Germany. Less than nine hours after the declaration of war, at 11 am on 3 September 1939, the Donaldson liner *Athenia* was sunk without warning by a U-boat off the west coast of Ireland. From that moment onwards, British merchant seamen were constantly in the front line in all quarters of the globe. For almost six years they faced, without flinching, their own private hell of torpedoes, bombs, shells and mines, all the while fending off their old arch-enemy the sea. Sorely pressed, and often tired near to death, they kept open Britain's tenuous lifelines, bringing in millions of tons of raw materials, oil, food, arms and ammunition, without which the country could not have survived. As always, their spirit was indomitable, their professionalism unchallenged. The price they paid for their bravery and dedication was horrendous: 2,426 ships lost, 29,180 men killed and countless hundreds maimed and wounded.

Since the North Atlantic was first crossed, this turbulent ocean has been an accursed place in the eyes of those who must sail it in pursuit of a living. It is a cold, unfriendly sea, often scourged by the most violent of storms, seldom at rest. In winter each swirling depression follows so closely on the heels of the other that they often merge to give an area of four million square miles of angry water, constantly seething beneath a canopy of sombre grey cloud unbroken from horizon to horizon. In summer the storms are muted and sporadic, but foolish is the seaman who would ignore their menace. It was on such a battlefield that the fiercest actions of the war at sea were fought.

Winston Churchill was to write in later years: 'The Battle of the Atlantic was the dominating factor all through the war. Never for one moment could we forget that everything happening elsewhere, on land, at sea, or in the air, depended ultimately on its outcome, and amid all other cares we viewed its changing fortunes day by day with hope or apprehension. Many gallant actions and incredible feats of endurance are recorded, but the deeds of those who perished will never be known. Our merchant seamen displayed their highest qualities, and the brotherhood of the sea was never more strikingly shown than in their determination to defeat the U-boat.'

For almost four years the battle did not go well for the merchant ships, scarcity of escorts and indifferent air-cover making the fight hopelessly one-sided. The German Type VIIC U-boats, of which 650 were thrown into the conflict, had a range of 8,500 miles, carried fourteen torpedoes, an 88mm deck gun and three anti-aircraft cannons, and were capable of maximum speeds of 17.3 knots on the surface and 7.6 knots submerged. Against them for much of the time were ranged only the 900-ton Flower-class corvettes of the Royal Navy and the Royal Canadian Navy, with a top speed of 15 knots, and armed with a single 4-inch gun and a handful of depth charges. Attacking on the surface at night, the U-boats were usually able to out-gun and out-manoeuvre these brave little ships.

In the early stages of the war there had been a gap of 1,700 miles in mid-Atlantic, where the merchant ships, huddled together in convoy like nervous cattle, were beyond the range of the escorts stationed on either side of the Atlantic. It was here that the most grievous slaughter took place, the unopposed U-boats falling upon the helpless merchantmen like packs of slavering wolves. Yet, despite the terrible losses they suffered, the convoys always clawed their way through, which says much for the ability of the merchant captains. Sailing in close company with other ships was totally alien to them; they would have preferred to take their chances alone, although the U-boats could out-run their tortoise-like commands, sometimes even when submerged.

With the fall of France in June 1940, the enemy's advantage increased, the new bases in the Bay of Biscay enabling even the small 500-ton coastal U-boats to operate up to 600 miles out in the Atlantic. Had Britain been able to gain the use of similar forward bases on the west coast of Ireland for her warships and aircraft, the odds would have been considerably shortened. But the Irish Republic, although heavily subsidised by Britain and dependent on supplies carried across the Atlantic in British ships, stubbornly refused to violate their neutrality in Britain's favour. By the end of 1940, Britain and her few remaining allies had lost 1,281 merchant ships, totalling 4.75 million tons. This total reached 7 million tons by June 1941, and there was worse to come.

Too many British merchantmen, the old tramps that made up the bulk of the fleet, were easy meat for the U-boats. In convoy, because of their characteristic lack of power, they were all too often unable to keep station, ending up as stragglers, to be picked off at leisure by the shadowing enemy. From 1940 onwards merchant ships began to be armed, but only with ancient, un-reliable 4-inch and 12-pounder guns left over from another war. The guns were manned at first by the merchant seamen them-selves, some of whom had undergone a three-day gunnery course. Later, gunners of the Royal Navy and Maritime

3

Anti-Aircraft Regiment, who formed the DEMS (Defensive Equipment Merchant Ships) force, took over. On the few occasions that they were able to bring their guns into action, the ships gave a good account of themselves, but all too often, struck by the unseen torpedo, they were on their way to the bottom before they could retaliate.

The men who manned the merchant ships, those who died, and those who lived to see the peace, were all quiet heroes, dedicated and uncomplaining. Yet, they were to receive scant recognition for the indispensable part they played in saving their country from extinction. They did not seek adulation, but the few civilian awards handed out – identical to those distributed annually for diligent service in industry and commerce ashore – were an insult to the men who had endured so much. It was certainly not the pay and conditions that kept them coming back to face the vicious onslaughts of the U-boats and the Focke-Wulfs voyage after voyage, year after year. At the best of times the sea is a dangerous, comfortless calling, demanding ten to twelve hours a day, seven days a week, and understood only by those who endure it. In 1942 the pay of an able seaman was £12 a month, that of a chief officer around £27. On top of this came a 'War Risk Bonus' of £10 a month, which was really only a shamefaced attempt to prevent the wages of a merchant seamen falling too far behind those ashore. It was a rotten war for those who kept the sea lanes open.

2

No Phoney War at Sea

At 11 o'clock on the morning of 3 September 1939 a sombre-voiced Prime Minister Neville Chamberlain informed the British people that they were at war with Germany. For the second time in a generation the gates of Armageddon had been reached.

While the war on land and in the air was to take months to break out into actual physical aggression, this was not the case at sea. Within ten hours of Chamberlain's announcement, the German submarine *U-30*, commanded by Kapitänleutnant Fritz-Julius Lemp, sank without warning the 13,581-ton Donaldson passenger liner *Athenia*, which presented no more threat to the Third Reich than did the women and children she was evacuating to America. The *Athenia* went down 250 miles to the north-west of Ireland with the loss of 112 passengers and crew. Lemp claimed to have mistaken the passenger ship for an armed merchant cruiser, but his action was to set the pattern for a long and dirty war against British and Allied merchant shipping. By the third week in November the U-boats had sunk sixty-six British merchant ships, with a heavy loss of life. There was no phoney war at sea.

The convoy system, which had proved so successful in the First World War, was put into operation from the outset, with only fast vessels of the calibre of the *Athenia* taking the risks alone. Many merchant captains disliked the convoy system, seeing it as a dangerous bunching together of their mainly slow and cumbersome charges. This dislike was understandable, since no man who commands a commercially-oriented ship can ever find complete peace of mind when he is hemmed in on all sides by others. Searoom is his most sought-after asset. He is also accustomed to taking sole responsibility for the actions of his ship, being answerable to God and the owner alone. To be forced to steam in company, at a regulated speed, on a course not of his choosing, and subject to the discipline of Navy men often many years his junior in age and experience was, is and always will be anathema to the captain of a merchant ship. But there are worse things in war than a temporary loss of independence. Few British masters refused to sail in a convoy in the Second World War, but there were many who were denied its protection through no fault of their own.

In winter, to voyage from Sunderland to Monaco is to move from darkness into light. It is a journey from a cold, damp land plagued by industrial smog to a warm Elysium of clean air and sparkling blue water set against a background of mountains clothed in pristine snow. The distance by sea is a mere 2000 miles, but the passage is not without its perils. The fog-shrouded sandbanks of the North Sea, the crowded narrows of the English Channel and the ponderous swells of the Bay of Biscay must all be safely negotiated before the first touch of a kinder climate is felt. Such was the prospect ahead of the crew of the steamer *Uskmouth* on a dreary day in November 1939.

The *Uskmouth*, built in 1928, was a small ship of only 2,483 tons gross and one of a fleet of three similar vessels owned by Richard Jones & Company. Manned by a crew of twenty-five, she was a typical short-sea tramp of the coal trade of the 1930s. Her paintwork was faded by constant washing to remove the grime of her employment, but she was, nevertheless, a personable little ship. In pre-war days the ships of R.W. Jones had sported white-painted superstructures which, in an era when most tramps, especially colliers, favoured a serviceable brown or buff, must have been regarded as nothing short of ostentation. Certainly the white upperworks were a never-ending headache for the chief officers, who were charged with the maintenance and cleanliness of these ships. As a concession to the war, now moving into its third month, the *Uskmouth*'s white paint had been covered by a drab grey, but she still retained her stark black hull. It was as though the phlegmatic men who ran this ship regarded the war as a passing annoyance that would soon go away, allowing them to resume their old way of life. That was not to be the case.

The *Uskmouth* left Sunderland at 2000 on the evening of 17 November loaded with 3,900 tons of coal for Monaco. She joined a coastal convoy, which would take her as far as Southend, in the Thames Estuary, where a larger convoy was forming for the deep-sea run down to the Straits of Gibraltar.

As far as the *Uskmouth*'s master, Captain H. Hunter, was concerned, his ship's presence in the coastal convoy was a mistake from the start. He was grateful for the protection offered by the Royal Navy, but despite the best efforts of the *Uskmouth*'s engineers, it proved impossible to reach or maintain the speed of 9 knots specified by the Convoy Commodore. Limping along at 8½ knots, she was a persistent straggler all the way down the North Sea.

At the very least, a North Sea passage in winter is a harrowing exercise for the shipmaster. The visibility is invariably poor and navigation marks few. For Captain Hunter, groping his way through the sandbanks paralleling the east coast of England, and at the same time attempting to remain part of an organized body of ships half a knot faster than his best, the 30-hour passage was a nightmare he had no wish to repeat. Having eventually arrived off Southend pier, Hunter made his apologies to the Convoy Commodore and the *Uskmouth* set out for Gibraltar on her own.

Forty-two hours later the collier was clear of the constrictions of the English Channel and heading out into open water, before turning to the south-west to cross the mouth of the Bay of Biscay. The weather was now fine, the visibility good and the long Atlantic swell muted. The heavily-laden ship had only a gentle corkscrewing motion, which would develop into a lazy roll when she turned beam-on to the swell. As he was sailing alone and unarmed, Hunter set his courses well clear of the land, first aiming for a point 100 miles west of Cape Finisterre, from where he intended to steam due south to the latitude of Gibraltar, before heading east. By remaining far out in the Atlantic for as long as possible, he hoped his ship would be safe from attack.

7

Given a functioning crystal ball, Hunter might well have decided to follow his old peacetime route, passing close to Finisterre and hugging the Spanish and Portuguese coasts on the way south. He did not, however, possess such a clairvoyant aid and was not to know, therefore, that in his chosen path lay *U-43*, under the command of Kapitänleutnant Wilhelm Ambrosius. The U-boat had already been blooded earlier in the month by sinking two British ships, the *Arlington Court* and the *Pensilva*, within a few days of each other. Ambrosius was now lying in wait for his third victim.

By 2300 on the night of the 25th the *Uskmouth* was abeam, but out of sight, of Cape Finisterre. A moderate swell was running, indicating a blow far out in the Atlantic, but the weather continued fine. Third Officer J. Robe, consoling himself that the last hour of his watch was passing, was keeping a lonely vigil in the port wing of the bridge, sweeping the horizon from time to time with tired eyes. Suddenly he snapped alert. An ominous-looking track of bubbles was racing in from port, angling towards the bow of the ship.

Robe threw himself into the wheelhouse, expecting at any moment to feel the shock of the explosion as the torpedo struck. Then, as his trembling fingers fumbled with the plug of the Captain's voicepipe, he saw through the forward window that the line of bubbles had crossed the bow from port to starboard and was disappearing into the night. It had been a very near miss.

Captain Hunter was on the bridge within seconds of answering the piercing whistle of the voice pipe. He was in doubt as to whether the track Robe had seen was that of a torpedo or the wash of a periscope, but there was no indecision in his action. Ordering the helmsman to put the wheel hard to starboard, he swung the ship through an arc of 90 degrees, putting her stern-on to his estimated position of the U-boat. At the *Uskmouth*'s top speed of 8½ knots, there was little chance of running away, even from a submerged U-boat, but Hunter intended to present the most difficult target possible for his attacker.

Hardly had the collier settled on her new course than Hunter glimpsed a phosphorescent track streaking in from the starboard bow. This time there was no mistaking the wake of an approaching torpedo.

Deciding it was too late to alter course to avoid the torpedo, Hunter's next thought was for his crew, may of whom would be fast asleep. Lunging for the lanyard of the steam whistle, he shattered the silence of the night with a succession of piercing blasts. As he did so, the torpedo passed close ahead, missing the *Uskmouth*'s bow by only a few feet.

In spite of the excitement of the moment, Hunter now found time to order his wireless operator to transmit the signal SSSS, followed by the ship's position. This, he hoped, would warn the Admiralty, and all other ships in the vicinity, that his vessel was being attacked by an enemy submarine. As this message was being tapped out, word was passed to the bridge that another torpedo had just crossed the stern from starboard to port. Hunter likened his position to that of a duck in a shooting gallery, as he repeated his earlier tactic, putting the helm hard to port to present his stern to the unseen attacker.

Wilhelm Ambrosius, crouched at the periscope of *U-43*, was seething with frustration. Due to bad luck and Hunter's evasive tactics, what should have been a simple copybook sinking of a small, unarmed merchantman was becoming a costly operation. He had already wasted three torpedoes, each carrying 360 kilos of high explosive and worth 40,000 Reichmarks apiece. Ambrosius decided it was time for the farce to end and gave the order to surface.

Hunter was in the act of steadying his ship on a south-easterly course when he saw the U-boat surface on his port quarter some 250 yards off. Through his binoculars he saw men running along her casing to the deck gun.

The shooting began almost at once, the first shells screaming between the *Uskmouth*'s masts to explode harmlessly in the sea beyond. Obviously the U-boat's first intention was to bring down the merchant ship's wireless aerials, thereby silencing her calls for help, which were still going out. Hunter, without even a light machine gun to defend his ship, could do no more than order his crew to stand by the boats while he did his best to spoil the U-boat's aim.

U-43's 88mm gun's crew were either poor shots or they were severely handicapped by the darkness, for they completely failed to carry away the *Uskmouth*'s top-masts or aerials. When they tired of this thankless task, they lowered their sights and began the grim work of the night. Shell after shell smashed into the collier's superstructure, the range being so short that it was impossible for the German gunners to miss.

It became clear to Hunter, still on the bridge of the *Uskmouth*, that the enemy was intent on destroying his ship with precious little regard for human life. Reluctantly, he swung the handle of the engine-room telegraph to stop and gave the order to abandon ship.

On receipt of the order from the bridge, the *Uskmouth*'s chief officer sprinted for the boat deck, where the rest of the crew, supervised by Third Officer Robe, were swinging out the port lifeboat. Shells were bursting all around them and, although there was no panic, the men worked with feverish haste. Boatswain Dowie climbed into the boat, knocked away the gripes and the Chief Officer gave the order to lower away. At that precise moment, a shell exploded on the boat deck sending a hail of shrapnel scything through the assembled men. Third Officer Robe and Able Seaman Davies were killed instantly and the forward fall of the lifeboat was severed. The bow of the boat plunged seawards, throwing Dowie into the water below. He was not seen again.

Captain Hunter now arrived on the boat deck and, amid the scream and crash of the shells, shepherded the dazed survivors towards the starboard lifeboat, which was still intact. This boat was lowered without further incident and the remaining twenty-two men of the *Uskmouth*'s crew piled aboard and cast off.

As there was still some way on the ship, the lifeboat drifted rapidly astern, passing close to the U-boat, which was now pumping shells into the abandoned merchantman as fast as her gun's crew could load and fire. Standing in the stern of the lifeboat, Hunter watched helplessly as his ship was pounded to pieces.

At 0125 on the morning of 26 November the *Uskmouth*,

burning fiercely, gave a last shudder, and slipped beneath the waves.

The actions of Wilhelm Ambrosius had been neither impressive nor humane. Faced with a small slow, and entirely defenceless merchant ship, he had, in direct contravention of the 1935 Geneva Convention, attempted to torpedo her without warning. Having failed miserably to do so, he then surfaced and opened fire without the *Uskmouth*'s crew being given a reasonable chance to abandon ship. Only by a miracle and the disciplined behaviour of that crew had very heavy casualties been avoided. As it was, three innocent seamen had died.

It may have been that Ambrosius felt his submarine threatened by the possible presence of British warships in the area; the convoy the *Uskmouth* had left off Southend was somewhere in the offing. More likely, the German commander was so enraged by the frustration of his torpedo attack by Captain Hunter's manoeuvres that all his more humane feelings were momentarily stifled. In any event it was a very hollow victory for Ambrosius and one unlikely to bring praise from the C-in-C U-boats, Admiral Karl Dönitz. In addition to three wasted torpedoes, *U-43* had expended nearly 100 rounds of 88mm amunition – and all this to sink a 2483-ton ship carrying nothing more vital than a few thousand tons of coal destined for a neutral country.

Having watched their ship sink and the U-boat motor off into the night, Hunter and the surviving members of his crew hoisted the sails of their crowded boat and set course for the Spanish coast, which they estimated to be 120 miles to the east. Fortunately, the weather held good and for the rest of that night and all next day they sailed steadily towards the land.

At 2300 on the 26th, having covered 110 miles, and when only 5 miles off Cape Villano, at the southern end of the Bay of Biscay, the lifeboat was sighted by the Italian steamer *Juventus* and Hunter and his men were picked up. Italy had then not yet entered the war, so the *Juventus* was able to land them at Ramsgate four days later. The survivors had spent only thirteen days at sea, but in that time had learned at first hand what they and their fellow British merchant seamen would have to face time and time again over the six years to follow.

11

The *Uskmouth* fiasco was the turning point in the fortunes of *U-43*, for then she went on to sink 100,000 tons of Allied shipping in the next three years or so. In one of her last actions of the war, then commanded by Oberleutnant Hans-Joachim Schwantke, she brought disgrace on herself by sinking one of her own, the German blockade runner *Doggerbank*, which Schwantke mistook for a British ship. Five months later, on 30 July 1943, and with no more sinkings to her credit, *U-43* was herself sunk by aircraft from the US Navy carrier *Santee*, when 260 miles south-west of the Azores. Wilhelm Ambrosius, who moved out of active U-boat service in October 1940 and was later promoted to Fregattenkapitän, survived the war and died in Germany in September 1955.

3

The Ship They Couldn't Sink

February is a bleak month in the winter cycle of northern Europe and never so bleak as in the windswept Orkney Islands. Separated from Scotland by the fast-running Pentland Firth and straddling the 59th parallel, this rugged archipelago of seventy-plus islands and rocks has little to offer, other than one of the finest landlocked anchorages in the world. Scapa Flow, 120 square miles of deep water sheltered from the Atlantic and the North Sea by the islands of Mainland to the north, South Ronaldsay to the east, and Hoy to the west, was home to the British Grand Fleet in the 1914-18 war and graveyard to the German High Seas Fleet in 1919. When another war came along, capital ships of the Royal Navy again made Scapa their base, and it was here, on 14 October 1939, that Günther Prien's *U-47* sank the battleship *Royal Oak* with the loss of 824 men.

The defences of Scapa Flow had been substantially improved, but the weather was as cheerless as ever when, at about 4 o'clock on the afternoon of Sunday 10 February, 1940 the British tanker *Imperial Transport* brought home her anchor and headed out into the Pentland Firth. The 12,427-ton motor vessel, owned by Houlder Brothers of London and commanded by Captain Walter Smail, was bound in ballast to Trinidad. The sun was already an hour below the horizon and the night wind keening through the firth was bitterly cold, penetrating even the thickest of woollen jumpers with ease. There was not a man among the *Imperial Transport*'s 43-man crew who did not look forward in

13

eager anticipation to the first caress of the warm Caribbean breeze, sad though they were to be leaving home.

The *Imperial Transport* was leaving behind her a Britain five months into the war, but quietly optimistic. Food rationing had been tightened, but no blood was yet running on the battlefields of France, and overhead the roar of British bombers signalled only the latest sortie to shower German cities with propaganda leaflets. In the pubs they still sang of hanging out the washing on the Siegfried Line, and such was the perceived absence of danger that more than half the children evacuated to the countryside from London and other big cities at the outbreak of war had returned home.

It was perhaps just as well that few people in Britain knew that the end of the 'phoney' war was imminent. Two million superbly trained and equipped German troops stood poised for attack on the frontiers of France, Belgium, Holland and Luxemburg, while the Luftwaffe was ready to carry out saturation bombing of the French airfields. Only a word from Hitler was needed to unleash the most vicious assault ever seen on the West. Providentially for the Allies, the weather on the continent had taken a turn for the worse, and Hitler, unwilling to move unless everything was in his favour, including the weather, had ordered the attack to be postponed until conditions improved.

While the war on land and in the air had yet to become a reality, at sea the fight continued unabated. In the month of January the U-boats and Hitler's 'ultimate weapon', the magnetic mine, had claimed another seventy British merchant ships, totalling 213,000 tons gross. Breaking through the ring of U-boats the Germans had thrown around the British Isles was a highly risky business, a thought which must have been uppermost in the mind of 42-year-old Captain Walter Smail as he rounded the southern point of Hoy and steered westwards through the Pentland Firth. It was a very dark night, with no moon and a fresh westerly breeze setting up a lumpy sea – ideal conditions for the *Imperial Transport* to slip out into the Atlantic unseen, but also providing equal cover for the marauding U-boats. Smail rang for full sea speed and the tanker, flying light, soon worked up to a respectable 12 knots.

14

At the time Dönitz's U-boats, operating from bases in North Germany were able to reach only as far as 15° W, some 300 miles out into the Atlantic, and Smail was anxious to clear the danger area as soon as possible. Beyond 15° W the only threat was likely to come from German surface raiders, and since the demise of the *Graf Spee*, brought about by British cruisers off the River Plate the previous December, this threat was very much diminished. At his present speed Smail estimated he would be reasonably safe from attack within thirty-six hours. Until then he must be on his guard. At midnight, abeam of Cape Wrath and clear of the Scottish coast, he began to zig-zag. As he did so, a dark shape was seen ahead, crossing the bows, setting nerves jangling on the bridge. The tension eased when a dim light was glimpsed as the stranger moved out onto the starboard bow, indicating she was a ship heading north. Whether she was friend or foe was not revealed. The remainder of the night passed without incident.

At first light on the 11th the *Imperial Transport* was 60 miles north-west of the Outer Hebrides and making steady progress to the west, riding easily on the long Atlantic swell. It was Smail's intention to hold this westerly course until clear of Rockall and then head south-westwards on a long great circle course to Trinidad, a distance of some 3,700 miles. A watery sun showed itself through the grey canopy of cloud on and off during the morning, long enough for sights to be taken, which at noon put the ship in 10° W longitude. And still the horizon remained empty. During the afternoon the tanker's recently fitted 4.7-inch stern gun was exercised, an operation which consisted mainly of the gun's crew – rank amateurs all of them – mustering and taking positions around the gun. The handful of shells carried would not run to a live shoot.

Night fell, bringing an icy wind laden with flurries of sleet and snow, but, with the *Imperial Transport* rapidly approaching the outer limits of the danger area, this did nothing to dampen the growing sense of optimism on her bridge. At 1830, two hours after sunset, drawing confidence from another black, moonless night, Captain Smail suspended the zig-zag and brought the ship round onto a course a little to the south of west. He anticipated

15

being clear of the island of Rockall soon after midnight, when it would be safe to alter onto a south-westerly course. By dawn on the 12th the war and all its nastiness would become just an unpleasant memory – for a month or two at least. However, anticipation is one thing; reality is often quite another.

Unknown to Walter Smail and his crew, slipping out into the North Atlantic under the cloak of darkness, a German submarine was close by. *U-53*, commanded by Korvettenkapitän Harald Grosse, was on a reciprocal course to the *Imperial Transport*, running on the surface and homeward bound at the end of her first, and largely unsuccessful, wartime patrol. Earlier in the day Grosse had sighted and sunk the 4000-ton Norwegian motor vessel *Snestad*, his first victim so far. One medium-sized ship sunk was not much to show for a long and uncomfortable cruise, but Grosse, short on fuel, had accepted he must now return to base without increasing his score. His lonely vigil in the cold, wet conning tower of the U-boat was beginning to seem pointless. Then he saw the long, dark shadow sliding through the night to port and his spirits rose. Through his night glasses he made out a familiar silhouette – long foredeck, bridge perched amidships, and a second block of accommodation grouped around the funnel right aft. He rubbed his frozen hands in anticipation. Fate had sent him a nice, fat tanker to round off the patrol.

Shortly after the change of watch, at 8 o'clock that night, Captain Smail, in accordance with his normal routine, was on his way up to the bridge to settle the ship down for the night. As he put his foot on the bottom rung of the starboard ladder leading up to the bridge, a torpedo crashed into the *Imperial Transport*'s port side and her well-ordered world exploded into chaos. She staggered, smoke swirled up from her bowels and a column of water and debris shot high in the air, then showered down on her bridge, drenching Smail as he took the ladder at a run.

When, breathless, he reached the wheelhouse, Smail felt his ship writhe in agony under him and he knew the explosion had broken her back. In seconds the deck beneath his feet began to open up as the forward section began to tilt and break away.

16

Fortunately, at this time of the day most of the *Imperial Transport*'s crew were in the after part of the ship, only Smail, his deck officers, radio officer and one or two ratings being forward. Smail shouted to them to evacuate the bridge and run for their lives.

With the screech of tearing metal in their ears, the men needed no urging and one by one they leapt across the widening gap opening up between the two separating halves of the ship. As the last man reached the safety of the catwalk leading aft to the stern, the bow section broke away and disappeared into the night. As it did, there was added to the awful cacophony the jangling of the engine-room telegraph bells as the stretching chains rang for full speed astern, before they finally snapped. The engineer on watch, deep below decks and unaware of what was happening, acknowledged the telegraph's ring and threw the engine astern. Luckily, Smail had by then reached the stern and was able to pass the word to stop the ship.

Fearful that the after section, now open to the sea, would soon sink, Smail then gave the order to abandon ship. The two lifeboats housed alongside the funnel were lowered, but in the confusion one of the falls of the port boat jammed, the boat tipped and two men were thrown into the sea. Smail took the starboard boat away to search for them – it was by then established that the missing men were the pumpman, Richard Edwards, and the second cook, Jack Williams – but the night was very dark, the wind was blowing hard and the heavy lifeboat was difficult to row. At one stage a light was seen on the water and shouts were heard, but, as Smail urged his men to row for the light, they saw the bow section of the *Imperial Transport*, still afloat, drifting down on them. By the time they had extricated themselves from this dangerous situation the light had gone and the men in the water were silent. Smail decided to return to the ship.

After an hour's hard pulling, the stern section of the tanker, which comprised about two-thirds of the original ship, was reached at midnight and Smail and his crew re-boarded. With the help of his chief engineer, Charles Swanbrow, Smail assessed the state of the ship and found that, although bowless and

17

bridgeless, she was seaworthy and saveable. Her engines were serviceable and, being built, like all tankers, with heavy frames and numerous bulkheads, her hull was watertight. Satisfied that, at the very least, the ship would not sink under them, the survivors lay down to wait out the night.

At daybreak on the 12th Smail was relieved to see his other lifeboat, under the command of Chief Officer J.W. Rees, lying to a sea anchor several miles off. He signalled her to come along-side and by mid-afternoon he had forty-one of his original crew on board. Now there were decisions to be made.

The torpedoing and subsequent break-up of the ship had been so sudden that no SOS was sent, so no early rescue could be expected. Therefore, two alternatives were open to the survivors: they could return to the lifeboats and attempt to sail home or stay with the ship and try to get her to port. Smail esti-mated their position as 200 miles to the west of the Hebrides and, given that they would be running before the wind, the first action was a distinct, if uncomfortable, possibility. However, Smail knew the North Atlantic well enough to be aware that the present fresh breeze might at any moment become a howling gale, in which no small boat could survive. As for staying with the damaged ship, she was highly vulnerable and there was a very real danger that the U-boat responsible for her predicament was still around, or another U-boat might appear on the scene. One more well-placed torpedo could send the tanker to the bottom, taking with her all those on board. Down through the years it has always been the opinion of seamen that their ship, so long as she will float, is the best lifeboat, and those on board the *Imperial Transport* held the same view. They opted to stay with the ship.

An inspection of the fore end of the ship showed a mass of twisted frames and broken plates where her bows had once been, but the forward bulkhead, as far as could be seen, was still intact. Smail had some doubts about whether this bulkhead would hold up against the pressure of the sea when going ahead, so he decided to try getting under way stern-first. But when the engine was run astern, the ship simply went round in circles. It had to be bow-first or nothing.

18

There was an additional complication, in that the charts and navigational instruments had all been lost with the bridge and Smail was faced by the prospect of having to navigate using a school atlas, a ruler and a spare compass that had an error on it in excess of 20 degrees. Furthermore, steering would be by the poop emergency gear, not the easiest of options at any time. Yet, in spite of all these deficiencies, at around 10 o'clock on the morning of the 13th the bowless *Imperial Transport* hoisted the Red Ensign at her stern and got under way. By noon she was making 3½ knots on a course as near to east as could be managed. That afternoon she passed her detached bow section, still afloat and drifting forlornly before the wind.

As had been anticipated, the tanker did not handle well under power and the two men on the wheel were engaged in a constant battle to hold her on course. The weather remained fair, however, and by noon on the 14th Smail estimated they had progressed 130 miles to the eastward. Given that their extra-ordinary good luck held, then another day might see them in sight of land. As it happened, their good fortune knew no bounds, for shortly before dark four British destroyers came over the horizon.

The chance meeting between this poor battered tanker and the Royal Navy was an occasion those on board the *Imperial Transport* would remember long after the war. But they were not home yet. Escorted by one of the destroyers, HMS *Kingston*, the tanker continued to make her slow way to the east, but soon the sudden deterioration in the weather that Captain Smail had lived in dread of for more than forty-eight hours became reality. Dawn on the 15th brought gale-force winds and rough seas which set the tanker pitching heavily. Fearing that the forward bulkhead would collapse under the strain, Smail reluctantly hove to. He then attempted to go stern-first, but, as before, the ship refused to steer. *Kingston* passed a tow wire across, but she was not powerful enough to move the drifting tanker.

The weather was steadily worsening and, as both ships were now dangerously exposed to any passing enemy, it was decided to abandon the *Imperial Transport* for the night, returning next morning. Transferring to the destroyer in darkness was a hazardous operation, but, thanks to the skill and determination of *Kingston*'s boats' crews, this was successful.

Daylight came on the 16th and there was no let-up in the weather, but the *Imperial Transport* was still afloat. When, later in the day, the fleet tugs *Forester* and *Buccaneer* arrived on the scene, Smail asked to be put back aboard his ship with sufficient crew to handle her. Unfortunately, the weather had become so bad that this was too risky, and *Kingston* steamed away, leaving the tugs to stand by the derelict tanker. As he watched his ship disappearing astern Smail was convinced he had seen the last of her. He was to be proved wrong.

The decimation of British merchant shipping by U-boat, mine and aircraft was continuing unabated and even part of a ship was considered worth saving. The *Imperial Transport* was towed in to the Clyde, where a new bow section was built and fitted, a relatively simple operation today, but in the 1940s a major feat of shipbuilding. Within six months the tanker was back at sea and ferrying more precious cargoes of oil across the Atlantic.

Captain Walter Smail was still in command of the *Imperial Transport* when, two years later, on 17 March, 1942, she joined Convoy ON 77, in ballast and bound for Curaçao. ON 77, a convoy of twenty-nine ships, typified the change that had taken place in the North Atlantic scene by 1942. Gone were the days of derisively-armed ships sailing alone. ON 77 was a first-rate convoy, escorted by two British destroyers, four Canadian corvettes, a Free French corvette and, with America now in the war, two US Coastguard cutters.

Sailing early on the morning of 17 March, ON 77 encountered thick fog in the North Channel and steamed at slow speed in line astern until clearing the land on the morning of the 18th, when the fog lifted. The convoy then formed up into six columns abreast, the *Imperial Transport* being fourth ship in the starboard column, not an ideal position for any ship. By then the weather was in an unusually benevolent mood, with calm seas and visibility described by the convoy commodore, Commodore K.E.L. Creighton, RNR, as 'extreme'. It was, in Creighton's opinion, this exceptional visibility that led to the convoy being sighted by a U-boat on the 19th. No doubt the fact that two ships

– ironically one of them the *Manchester Division*, which carried the Commodore – persisted in making excessive smoke did not help. Radio signals picked up by MF/DF indicated that the U-boat was shadowing the convoy and reporting its position at intervals.

As it happened, nothing came of the perceived threat, and for the next five days ON 77 continued on a south-westerly course in fair weather and averaging 9¼ knots. It now seemed reasonable to assume the worst of the danger was behind them and when Captain Smail left the bridge of the *Imperial Transport* soon after midnight on 24 March he looked forward to sleeping easy. In just over forty-eight hours the convoy was due at the dispersal point to the south of Newfoundland and thereafter the tanker would be free to proceed independently and at full speed. A week later they would reach Curaçao.

The night was fine, with a moderate wind and sea, good visibility and a half-moon that shed a reassuring light whenever it appeared from behind the clouds. It was during one of the brief dark periods that the *Imperial Transport*, for the second time in her career, found herself at the wrong end of a U-boat's periscope. At 0120 on the 25th Kapitänleutnant Otto Ites, commanding *U-94*, fired a fan of four torpedoes.

Two of Ites' torpedoes missed, but one hit the tanker in her forward hold and another slammed into her port side between her Nos 2 and 3 cargo tanks, in almost the exact spot where she had been wounded two years earlier. This time the *Imperial Transport* did not break her back, but took a heavy list to port. Several men were injured and the steering gear was damaged. Captain Smail ordered the boats away.

The French corvette *Aconit* moved in quickly to pick up the *Imperial Transport*'s crew and then circled the crippled tanker until daylight. At 0630 the corvette closed in again and lowered a boat, which took Smail and Chief Engineer Swanbrow back to their ship. They found her with a 15 degree list to port, with the foredeck awash, but, once again, her engines were unharmed.

Having been through all this agony before, Smail and Swanbrow might have been forgiven if they had then thrown in the towel and accepted that, this time, the *Imperial Transport*

21

must be left to her fate. But they were men who did not accept defeat easily. They returned to the corvette, called for volunteers and next morning re-boarded the tanker with Second Engineer Alfred Broom, Fourth Engineer Karlis Malins, two engine-room ratings and two officers and a commissioned mechanician from the corvette HMS *Mayflower*. Steam was raised, the pumps started and at 1530 on the 26th the *Imperial Transport* was again under way and heading for St John's Newfoundland, escorted by the *Mayflower*. She reached port and, when her battered hull was once again made good, returned to sea and carried on with her vital task of supplying oil for the British war effort. She survived the war.

The two U-boats involved in the attacks on the *Imperial Transport* did not enjoy her extraordinary good fortune. Only twelve days after she had torpedoed the British tanker, on 23 February, 1940, *U-53* was caught by the destroyer HMS *Gurkha* to the south of the Faeroes and sunk. *U-94* fared somewhat better, in that she survived for another five months after her brush with ON 77, being finally run to ground and despatched near the West Indies on 28 August, 1942 by HMCS *Oakville* and aircraft of the 92nd US Squadron. Harald Grosse and Otto Ites were lost with their boats.

4

The 'Happy Time' Begins

There were few signs of elation in Britain in June 1940. The bulk of the BEF, nearly 340,000 men, had been successfully evacuated from the beaches of Dunkirk, but they had come home exhausted, demoralized and without much of their arms and equipment. In war defeat is defeat, no matter by which name you choose to call it. Italy had declared war on 10 June, and, with the rest of Europe under subjugation and the Americans apparently uninterested in events across the Atlantic, Britain was alone, except for the support of her dominions overseas. But vast and plenteous though those territories might be, the sea lanes joining them to the mother country were vulnerable and increasingly threatened.

The evacuation from Dunkirk had cost the Royal Navy twenty-five destroyers either sunk or seriously damaged and, with Hitler's invasion barges now massing on the other side of the Channel, there were precious few escorts left over for convoy work. It was not uncommon to see twenty or thirty merchant ships escorted by a single armed tug or a minesweeper, or with no other protection than the Admiralty's blessing. In the month of June 1940 Britain's merchant fleet lost sixty-one ships, totalling 282,560 tons, to enemy action.

For the U-boats this was the beginning of their 'Happy Time', when men like Otto Kretschmer, Günter Prien and Englebert Endrass were to reap a fearful harvest among the almost defence-less merchant ships. Matching sinking for sinking with these seasoned aces was the young Frits-Julius Lemp, who had already earned a place in history by torpedoing the *Athenia* in the opening hours of the war. Following the outcry over the sinking of the passenger ship, Lemp was recalled to Germany for a severe reprimand, but he was back in the North Atlantic by the end of December in command of his old boat, *U-30*. By the third week in June 1940 Lemp was patrolling the south-western approaches to the British Isles, having added another eleven ships to his score, none of them carrying passengers, but all sunk without warning.

Since her maiden voyage in March 1929 the Evan Thomas, Radcliffe & Company's steamer *Llanarth* had been engaged on a triangular trade, carrying coal from South Wales to the Mediterranean, then in ballast to South America, and home again with grain. There was plenty of hard work in this trade for the *Llanarth*'s crew, with holds to be cleaned after the discharge of the coal, shifting boards to be rigged for the grain – all this on the ballast passage – but the round-voyage was reasonably short and the weather fair for much of the time. Inevitably, the war had put an end to this agreeable routine. Mid-June 1940 saw the 5053-ton *Llanarth* in Freetown, about to embark on the last leg of an 11,000-mile passage from Australia. Although the voyage was long, much of it had been spent far away from the wearying tensions of the war. It was a welcome change of atmosphere for Captain John Parry and his 35-man crew.

Sailing from Freetown on 12 June, the *Llanarth* set out unescorted for Falmouth, nearly 3000 miles to the north. She was riding very low in the water, her holds filled to capacity with 7,980 tons of flour from Melbourne. For much of the passage northwards Captain Parry anticipated no problems, other than the normal day-to-day worries that always confront a shipmaster. His ship was slow, but well-armed for a merchantman, having, in addition to the usual machine guns, a 4-inch anti-submarine gun and a 12-pounder high/low angle gun for use against aircraft. However, anxious to minimize the risk to his vessel, Parry reached far out into the Atlantic, adhering strictly to the route given to him by the Naval Control in Freetown. As an added precaution, he followed a timed zig-zag pattern of course by day and in bright moonlight in order to confuse any

24

shadowing U-boats. Only in complete darkness did he steer a straight course.

On the night of the 27th, having steamed 2,700 lonely miles without incident, the *Llanarth* was in the Western Approaches, some 250 miles south-west of Land's End. Being now in higher latitudes, darkness was slow to fall and it was 2000 before Parry deemed it safe to discontinue zig-zagging for the night. Having seen the ship settled down on her course, he left the Third Officer in charge of the bridge and went below. Parry again visited the bridge at 2300 and spent some time checking that all was well. By then the night had taken on a deep, comforting blackness and it seemed, for the time being at least, that the *Llanarth* was alone on an empty sea. However, she was now entering the English Channel and Parry remained on the bridge for another two hours before he decided it was safe for him to risk putting his feet up on his dayroom settee. He went below again.

Kapitänleutnant Lemp calculated he had reached the position BF 4192 on his German Naval grid system chart, which put *U-30*, in terms of latitude and longitude, in 47° 30' N 10° 30' W. Lemp considered that he was now well situated to monitor the approaches to both the English Channel and the St George's Channel. He was confident that, sooner or later, a British convoy would come his way. But Lemp did not have to wait for a convoy, with its attendant dangers from escorting warships. Shortly after midnight the unmistakable outline of a heavily-laden merchant ship was seen on the horizon. After satisfying himself that the ship was alone, Lemp manoeuvred *U-30* into an advantageous position and at two minutes past one on the morning of 28 June gave the order to fire.

Ideally, Lemp would have wished his torpedo to strike the merchant ship squarely in her engine-room, thereby rendering her without power and flooding the largest single compartment in the ship. Unfortunately – or fortunately, depending on which side you should wish to favour – Lemp had miscalculated. The 21-inch torpedo slammed into the *Llanarth*'s hull some 50 feet aft of the engine-room, in the region of her No. 5 hold. It exploded with a deafening roar.

John Parry, resting in his dayroom before facing the difficulties

25

of the Channel passage, was thrown into the air by the blast. For a few moments he lay dazed on the deck of his cabin, his nostrils filled with the acrid stench of burnt cordite. When his mind cleared, and the fact that his ship had been torpedoed became plain, he got to his feet, staggered across to the small safe and hurriedly removed the ship's confidential papers and books. These included Admiralty secret codes, signals and prearranged routes, which Parry knew must not fall into enemy hands. Stuffing the books and papers into the weighted canvas bag supplied for such an emergency, he stepped out onto the deck. The sight that greeted him there was more terrible than he had feared. The whole of the deck appeared to be in flames, the ship was listing to port and visibly settling by the stern. Without hesitation, Parry hurled the weighted bag into the sea. There would be no further need for Admiralty instructions now.

Taking the bridge ladder two steps at a time, Parry burst into the wheelhouse to find its occupants, the Third Officer and the helmsman of the watch, still in a state of shock. First giving the order to stop the engine, Parry sent the helmsman aft to organize a fire party, its first priority to attempt to keep the flames away from the 4-inch magazine on the poop deck. Turning to the Third Officer, Parry instructed him to clear away the lifeboats. While there might still be a chance of saving the ship, he was prudent enough to prepare for the worst.

After what seemed like hours, but was in reality only minutes, Parry was joined on the bridge by his chief and second officers, both of whom had been off watch and asleep when the torpedo struck. Parry sent the Second Officer to take charge of the lifeboats and signalled the Chief Officer to follow him aft.

The scene that met the two men on the after deck was chaotic and frightening, but perhaps not as hopeless as Parry had expected. The tarpaulins, hatch boards and beams were missing from No.5 hatch, blown skywards by the explosion, and the cargo in the hold was well alight. Other fires had broken out on the poop deck among the piles of dunnage wood stowed there and, just as he had feared, the flames were licking dangerously close to the 4-inch magazine. The list to port was now more pronounced, but the *Llanarth* did not yet appear to be in

26

immediate danger of sinking. If the fire could be brought under control, there might still be a chance of saving her. But as Parry and his chief officer set about organizing the fight, all steam pressure was suddenly lost in the engine-room and the *Llanarth*'s fire pumps ground to a halt, leaving the hoses limp and waterless in the hands of the fire party. Parry walked over to the ship's side rail and looked down into the sea. The water was now less than 3 feet from the deck. Sadly, he gave the order to lower the boats.

Since shortly after being awoken by the explosion, the *Llanarth*'s wireless operator, following the prearranged emergency routine, had been attempting to get away a distress signal, but without success. His transmitter appeared to have been damaged by the blast of the explosion and, although he repeatedly tapped out the call for help on all possible frequencies, he received no reply. He reported the situation to Parry, who called in at the wireless room after leaving the blazing after deck. Parry asked the operator to keep sending until it was time to abandon ship. Sparks went back to his key, but could make no contact with either ship or shore station.

Despite the heavy swell running, both *Llanarth*'s lifeboats were lowered and pulled clear of the ship without too much difficulty. Reluctant to leave his stricken ship, and perhaps hoping for a miracle, Parry held the two boats together close to the leeward of the *Llanarth*. By the light of the flames he examined her hull, trying to assess the extent of the damage, but whatever ghastly hole had been torn in his ship was now well below the waterline and beyond plugging. It was a gaping wound that would very soon bring about her demise. After a while, mindful of the danger of exploding ammunition, Parry withdrew both boats to a safe distance and waited for the end.

The wind and sea were now rising and most of the occupants of the two lifeboats were soon helpless with seasickness. After about twenty minutes the flames on the *Llanarth* seemed to be dying down and Parry began to give thought to re-boarding. But it was only the waves quenching the fires as they washed over the sinking ship. Then, less than three quarters of an hour after *U-30*'s torpedo had ploughed into her, the *Llanarth* gave up the fight and sank.

Throughout the rest of the hours of darkness Parry tried to keep the two boats together, but with the weather fast deteriorating as a depression moved in from the Atlantic, he was unable to do so. When daylight came, just after 0400 on this summer's morning, the Chief Officer's boat was nowhere to be seen. Anxious to regain contact with the rest of his crew, Parry put his own boat stern-on to the waves, so that it would ride more comfortably, and then set his men to rowing easily, just maintaining steerage way on the boat. A sharp lookout was kept for the other boat and at about 0800, with the sun climbing rapidly behind the gathering clouds, what looked like a sail was sighted on the horizon. Parry was at once tempted to row towards it, but had second thoughts. The 'sail' could just as easily be the conning tower of a submarine and without binoculars he could not be sure. He decided not to take the risk of investigating. In the event, he probably made a wise decision, for, unknown to him, a number of U-boats, attracted by reports of a convoy inward bound from the south, were in the area.

Over the following twenty-four hours the weather worsened, the wind gradually working up to gale force. In their rolling cockleshell of a boat, Parry and his men struggled to step the mast, hoping to be able to hoist sail and run before the south-westerly wind in the general direction of the land. But the movement of the boat became so violent that it proved impossible to raise the mast and they were forced to continue rowing. By the morning of the 29th every man in the boat was exhausted, their hands blistered and bleeding, their back muscles on fire. Then, slowly, the wind began to drop and, calling on their last reserves of strength, they heaved the mast up and hoisted sail.

All that day, and for much of the following night, they sailed north-eastwards before a light wind, but a ship's lifeboat being heavy and having none of the sailing qualities of a yacht, their progress towards the land was painfully slow. At dawn on Sunday 30 June, they ran out of wind altogether and lay becalmed. There was little Parry could do now except await the passage of events. He calculated that the boat had moved far enough to the eastward to be in the path of ships bound in and out of the Irish Sea and the English Channel, and there was also the possibility of being sighted by patrolling British aircraft. If no rescue came, they would continue sailing towards the land when sufficient wind arose again.

The passage of events proved far quicker than Parry had anticipated. Within an hour of the wind falling away smoke was sighted on the horizon to the north. As the men in the boat watched, their spirits rising, the single wisp of smoke became two, then a dozen. Soon a collection of masts and funnels began to rise above the horizon. Parry rallied his men and once again the oars dipped and the boat crept slowly through the water, its bows pointed hopefully towards the ships in the north.

Although the survivors pulled with a will, it soon became obvious, even to the most optimistic among them, that the convoy, which appeared to be on a north-easterly course, would pass too far off to sight their small boat. Desperation heightened by fear gave way to grim determination and the heavy oars dipped faster and faster. When, at last, the boat began to make appreciable headway through the water, they were overjoyed to see a Sunderland flying boat heading in their direction. At first the big aircraft failed to see them and their cheers turned to curses. But then the Sunderland came back and circled low over the lifeboat, before flying off in the direction of the convoy. The oars were taken up with new enthusiasm and, as the convoy had altered course – presumably on the next leg of its zig-zag pattern – the lifeboat and the columns of ships drew slowly together. Soon an escort vessel was seen to break away and steam towards them with a foaming bow-wave. By 0800 the *Llanarth*'s boat was bumping alongside the Flower-class corvette HMS *Gladiolus*, and Captain John Parry and his men were climbing the scrambling nets to safety and a hearty breakfast, courtesy of the Royal Navy. However, their ordeal was not yet over.

5

The Rescue Ship

Of all the ships in Convoy SL 36 there was at least one most unsuited to be in company. The 5218-ton *Beignon*, owned by Morel Ltd, built in 1939, was outwardly a conventional 5-hatch cargo ship of her day, but in reality a diesel-engined motorship with a top speed of 12 knots. That made her a good 3 knots faster than the majority of elderly coal-fired steamers that dominated the ranks of SL 36, which was to make the passage north to British waters at a leisurely 7½ knots. In hindsight, it seems clear that, had the *Beignon* used her superior speed to sail independently she might well have survived to end her days in a shipbreaker's yard some thirty years later. As it turned out, her presence in the ranks of SL 36 drew her into an unfortunate saga of coincidence and violence that was to end in tragedy on a fine summer's morning in July 1940.

SL 36 left the busy anchorage of Freetown harbour at 1300 on 16 June. Steaming in line astern, the ships passed close to the tall lighthouse on Cape Sierra Leone, skirted the dangerous Carpenter Rock and formed up in orderly columns for the long passage north. The convoy was in two sections, ships bound for Liverpool, Glasgow and the Bristol Channel being on the port side, while those heading for the East Coast ports and London were to starboard. The Convoy Commodore was in the 13,376-ton Blue Star cargo liner *Avelona Star*, while protection of a sort was provided by HMS *Dunvegan Castle*, an armed merchant cruiser of 15,007 tons. The *Beignon*, being at the time of sailing uncertain of her port of discharge, was assigned to position No.13, third ship in the outer column on the port side of the convoy. Neither the numerical designation nor the exposed position of the ship were to the liking of the more superstitious on board.

The convoy's northward route lay between the bulge of Africa and the Cape Verde Islands, and then in a long gentle curve towards the Western Approaches. Although she was burdened with 8,816 tons of wheat, the *Beignon* had no difficulty in keeping station as SL 36 zig-zagged through the tropics. The weather was fine and was expected to remain so until the Western Approaches were reached. Then the unpredictable British maritime climate would take over, sure to bring with it, even in these months of high summer, anything from dense fog to a howling gale. However, confident in his ship and his crew, the *Beignon*'s master, Captain W.J. Croome, was content to take each day as it came.

In the early hours of the morning of 28 June, when SL 36 was roughly abeam of Lisbon, 550 miles to the north of the convoy, the *Llanarth* was on fire and sinking, after being torpedoed by Frits-Julius Lemp in *U-30*. No word of this attack reached SL 36, which was unwittingly sailing into a trap set by Admiral Karl Dönitz. Lemp was to be joined by Korvettenkapitän Hans-Gerrit von Stockhausen in *U-65*, Kapitänleutnant Heinz Scheringer in *U-26* and Kapitänleutnant Wilhelm Ambrosius, who had despatched the unfortunate *Uskmouth* the previous September, in *U43*. The first of Dönitz's wolf packs was gathering.

By the 30th of the month SL 36 was crossing the Bay of Biscay, having covered 2,500 miles of its long trek north unmolested. Its sole escort, HMS *Dunvegan Castle*, had been joined by destroyers and corvettes of Western Command, while Sunderlands of RAF Coastal Command kept watch overhead. There was a growing air of confidence in the ranks of the convoy. That morning, as breakfast was being passed up from the galleys, the ships were witness to the rescue of the *Llanarth*'s survivors by the corvette *Gladiolus*. This was a welcome break in the monotony of the long passage, but it proved to be a bad omen for the day ahead.

At three minutes past noon, von Stockhausen in *U-65* opened up the score for the wolf pack by torpedoing the 5802-ton cargo liner *Clan Ogilvy*. The fragile peace of the day was then shattered by the thunder of exploding depth charges as the escorts raced into action. Their prompt retaliation prevented von Stockhausen from administering the *coup de grâce* to the *Clan Ogilvy*, which, although damaged forward, was still afloat. The other U-boats also held back and the convoy, now on full alert, proceeded warily on its way.

Late that afternoon, when about 200 miles to the north-west of Cape Finisterre, Captain Croome received orders to take the *Beignon* to Newcastle to discharge her cargo of wheat. This led to the Commodore directing the *Beignon* to change her position to the starboard wing of the convoy, joining the other ships bound for the East Coast. This manoeuvre, which entailed pulling out of the ranks and steaming round astern of the convoy to take up position at the rear of the starboard outer column, was completed by 1800. When she was in position, the Commodore signalled the *Beignon* instructing her to act as rescue ship in the event of a night attack by the U-boats. As a 'tail-ender' with a good turn of speed, the *Beignon* was well suited for this work.

The *Beignon* was called upon to act out her new role far sooner than expected and, ironically, her first customer was the Commodore's own ship. At 2115, in the last of the twilight, the *Avelona Star*, steaming in the lead of the starboard column, and about 1 mile ahead of the *Beignon*, erupted in a cloud of smoke and flame. Wilhelm Ambrosius in *U-43* had fired the first shot of the night.

When the smoke cleared, the Blue Star ship could be seen to be listing to starboard and settling slowly in the water. While the rest of the convoy dispersed and the escorts went into their defensive routine, Croome brought the *Beignon* around and raced for the crippled ship. Over the next two hours, although under constant threat of being torpedoed, the rescue ship lay hove-to close to the sinking *Avelona Star*, picking up eighty-three of her 85-man crew. The remaining two men were rescued by the *Dunvegan Castle*.

As passengers in HMS *Gladiolus*, Captain John Parry and his men were treated to a grandstand view of the attack on SL 36.

Soon after the *Avelona Star* was hit the corvette left the convoy, with the object of landing the *Llanarth*'s survivors at Plymouth, but she had not pulled more than a couple of miles ahead of the other ships when *U-26* put a torpedo into the United Africa Company's *Zarian*. *Gladiolus* was immediately ordered to rejoin the other escorts, who then turned their fury on *U-26*. She was finally tracked down and sunk by the destroyer *Rochester*. Heinz Scheringer and his crew were taken prisoner. Meanwhile, the *Zarian* was still afloat and limping along in the rear of the convoy.

After playing her part in the attack on *U-26*, *Gladiolus* was detailed to stand by the *Zarian* for the night. Next morning she was ordered to escort the *Clan Ogilvy*, which, with her bows blown off, was attempting to make port stern-first. Thus Parry and his men were condemned to spend another forty-eight hours aboard the crowded corvette before being landed in Plymouth on the morning of 3 July. There Parry received the good news that the *Llanarth*'s other lifeboat had been picked up.

The *Beignon* had been left far behind the convoy as she worked to rescue the crew of the *Avelona Star*. As soon as this was finished, at 2215 on the 30th, Croome, uncomfortably aware of the vulnerability of his ship, made all speed in an effort to catch up with SL 36. As a precaution against a surprise attack, he used an unorthodox zig-zag pattern and kept his guns, a 4-inch, 12-pounder and an array of machine guns, continuously manned, this with the help of some of the *Avelona Star*'s gunners. Thus prepared, Croome pushed on through the night, hopeful of rejoining the convoy soon after daylight on 1 July. He was completely unaware that *U-30* was trailing along in the wake of SL 36.

Dawn came early on the 1st, the sky to the eastwards beginning to lighten around 0330. The promise of a warm sun rising on a fine day breathed new life into the *Beignon*'s 4-inch gun's crew standing-to on her poop deck. The unspoken fears of the night faded away and the men looked forward with confidence to being under the wind of the convoy's escorts within a few hours.

Daylight brought little comfort to Fritz-Julius Lemp in *U-30* who had spent the night on the surface astern of SL 36. Mindful of the threat posed by patrolling enemy aircraft, Lemp was obliged to take his boat down to periscope depth as soon as the sky began to pale. With her speed reduced to a crawl under water and her battery power draining away with every hour that passed, *U-30* seemed most unlikely to add to her score that day. Which was why Lemp could scarcely believe his luck when he saw the merchant ship coming up astern with a bone in her teeth.

At 0345 a torpedo tracked across the *Beignon*'s stern from port to starboard, rudely jerking the 4-inch gun's crew out of their early morning reverie. The gunlayer dived for the bridge telephone. Twenty minutes later Captain Croome, who had reached the bridge soon after the telephoned warning from the poop, saw a second torpedo narrowly miss his ship. It could only be a matter of time before his unseen attacker found the right deflection.

The third torpedo followed close on the heels of the second and was not seen from the bridge, but resulted in a violent explosion that seemed to lift the ship bodily and stop her dead in her tracks.

The *Beignon* had been hit on her starboard side, about 150 feet from the bow. She immediately began to settle by the head and it was at once obvious to Croome that she had little time left. It was unnecessary for him to give the order to abandon ship. His crew, assisted by the *Avelona Star* survivors, alerted by the opening attack half an hour earlier, were already launching the boats and rafts. With a total of 116 men to evacuate, they knew time was of the essence. Croome remained on the bridge until all boats and rafts were clear of the ship, then went below to check the accommodation. Having satisfied himself that no one else was still on board, he slipped on his lifejacket and returned to the bridge, determined not to leave his ship until all hope of saving her had gone. He did not have long to wait. At 0423, just eight minutes after Lemp's torpedo struck home, the *Beignon* dipped her broken bow into the swell for the last time and sank. Croome went down with her.

After what seemed like an eternity, Croome was able to break free of the suction created by the sinking ship and kicked his way to the surface. Luckily for him, the sea was calm and within a few minutes he found himself clinging to a floating spar in company with one of his young apprentices.

With his head only a foot or so above water, Croome's horizon was strictly limited. Try as he may, he failed to catch sight of any of the *Beignon*'s lifeboats or rafts and was forced to accept that the possibility of being seen and picked up was very remote. The ship had been some 13 miles astern of the convoy, and out of sight, when she was hit and it was unlikely that the explosion had been heard by any of the other ships. Worse still, her wireless transmitter had been damaged by the shock and no SOS had gone out. The likelihood of a search being made for survivors of a ship which was probably not known to be sunk was not worth considering.

Croome and his young companion were saved, indirectly, as a result of the *Clan Ogilvy* being torpedoed by Hans-Gerrit von Stockhausen on the previous day. Almost two hours after the *Beignon* went down the destroyer *Vesper* and HMS *Gladiolus*, who had been ordered to stand by the damaged Clan liner during the night, came up at full speed, hurrying to rejoin SL 36. Alert lookouts in *Vesper* spotted the two men in the water and they were soon safe on board the destroyer. Thirty-six hours later, they were landed in Plymouth, along with the *Llanarth*'s survivors brought in by *Gladiolus*. Of the rest of the *Beignon*'s crew two were lost and one died after rescue. Five men of the *Avelona Star* also lost their lives when the *Beignon* was torpedoed.

U-30 paid for the sinking of the *Llanarth* and *Beignon* later in the year when she was damaged and had to be abandoned by her crew. Swift action by a Royal Navy boarding party secured the U-boat before she sank. Lemp was not in command of *U-30* at the time. He was to die in *U-110* while attacking Convoy OB 318 in the North Atlantic on 9 May 1941. Forced to surface by depth charges dropped by the corvette HMS *Aubrietia*, *U-110* was fired on by the destroyers *Broadway* and *Bulldog*, and eventually boarded and captured, only to sink eleven hours later. *Aubrietia* picked up some survivors from the U-boat. Fritz-Julius Lemp was not among them.

35

6

Indian Ocean Raider

In February 1941 British land forces, pushing north from the Kenyan border, advanced into Italian Somaliland sweeping all before them. The Italians, having little stomach for the fight, disappeared into the barren hinterlands of Ethiopia, leaving behind them vast quantities of stores, arms and ammunition. In their hurry to depart, Mussolini's disillusioned men also abandoned a prisoner of war camp, of which they had good reason to be ashamed. When British troops entered the camp, 60 miles to the north of Mogadishu, they found 194 Allied merchant seamen living in the depths of privation and degradation. Dirty, half-starved, racked by dysentery and with their clothes in tatters, the men were survivors of ships sunk by the German raider *Atlantis*. Thirty-eight were from the British steamer *King City*, which had gone down under the guns of the *Atlantis* more than six months earlier.

The idea of using armed merchant ships to attack the enemy's shipping was born in the First World War when Germany's Imperial Navy was securely bottled up in its own ports by the Royal Navy. On 21 December 1916 the German windjammer *Seeadler* (Sea Eagle), commanded by Graf Felix von Luckner, slipped past the British blockade of the North Sea disguised as the Norwegian barque *Hero*, bound for Australia. Concealed beneath her deck cargo of timber were two 4.2-inch guns and below her after-deck planking was a powerful auxiliary engine. By the time she was shipwrecked in the Society Islands seven months later, the *Seeadler* had sailed 30,000 miles and accounted for fourteen Allied merchant ships worth in the region of £6 million. The merchant surface raider had arrived.

The *Atlantis*, commanded by Kapitän-zur-See Bernhard Rogge, bore no resemblance to the *Seeadler*, yet she was her direct descendant. Built in 1922 for the Hansa Line of Bremen as the *Goldenfels*, she was of 7,862 tons, with a top speed of 18 knots. Commandeered by the German Navy in 1939, she put into Kiel, where she was equipped with six 5.9-inch guns, four torpedo tubes, a number of light and heavy machine guns, ninety-three mines and two Arado spotter planes. All these accoutrements of war were hidden away behind portable screens or below decks, so that the *Atlantis* retained the innocent appearance of her former days as a cargo liner. Although her 5.9s were forty years old, she was, in reality, a force to be reckoned with, all the more dangerous for her ability to pose as a harmless neutral merchantman. Manned by 347 naval personnel, the *Atlantis* set sail from Kiel on 31 March 1940, her aim to create the maximum possible havoc amongst Allied shipping in the Indian Ocean.

Six weeks after the *Atlantis* broke through the British blockade, the 4744-ton *King City*, taken into service as a collier for the Royal Navy, left Cardiff with 5000 tons of coal on board, bound for Singapore via the Cape of Good Hope.

No seaman worthy of the name will ever admit to more than just a touch of sadness when he quits his home port on a long voyage. To do so would undermine that inner determination which, voyage after voyage, sustains him in the swift transformation from life ashore to life at sea, to move from the relaxed atmosphere of home and family into the regulated, isolated world of a ship. In time of war, with the everyday dangers of seagoing increased one hundredfold, the crossing of the line is even more difficult. The *King City*'s four apprentices were young enough not to be troubled by such mundane problems when their ship left Cardiff in mid-July 1940. Lesley Bayley, Alexander Davidson, Aubrey Radford and Leslie Thomas were all, give or take a month or two, seventeen years old, fresh-faced, open-minded and filled with enthusiasm for the voyage ahead. Wonderful new worlds were waiting for them over the horizon. For Captain Harry Marshall, commanding the 12-year-old *King*

City, on the other hand, the forthcoming voyage held no such delights. Ahead of him lay a run of 11,700 miles, at least forty-six days at sea, during which, unescorted for much of the time, his ship would be constantly exposed to danger. His current information was that the U-boats were then sinking fourteen British ships a week, their sphere of action extending south to Sierra Leone and beyond. It seemed quite likely that some of the U-boats, attended by supply ships, would soon be operating off the Cape of Good Hope, where their pickings would be rich. As for the Indian Ocean, which the *King City* would have to cross alone, there was strong talk of one, perhaps two, German surface raiders at large. These would pose a very real threat, against which the *King City* could muster only an ancient 4-inch gun mounted on her stern.

Contrary to Captain Marshall's fears, the *King City* steamed south through the Atlantic without as much as a glimpse of the enemy. Rounding the Cape of Good Hope in the first week of August, Marshall set course to pass well south of the southern approaches to the Mozambique Channel, knowing that this channel, traditional route of ships bound to and from the Cape to India and Suez, would be closely watched by any German raiders and U-boats abroad in the Indian Ocean. Marshall did not breathe easily until he had passed south of Mauritius and had settled the *King City* on the long north-westerly leg across the Indian Ocean towards the Malacca Straits, gateway to Singapore and the Far East.

Since leaving German waters at the end of March the *Atlantis* had already more than justified the confidence placed in her by Admiral Raeder. On her way south she had evaded detection by British warships, had fallen in with and sunk the 6199-ton merchantman *Scientist* off Angola on 3 May and had success-fully laid her deadly cargo of mines off Cape Agulhas on the 18th. The portents for her continued success were good. During the first three months, moving deeper into the Indian Ocean all the time, she sank four more Allied ships, each one despatched quickly and cleanly without damage to herself.

Late on the night of 24 August the *Atlantis* was idling some 180 miles to the north-east of Rodrigues Island, a tiny tropical paradise lying 800 miles to the east of Madagascar. The weather was anything but idyllic, for the southern winter was not yet done and the wind was high, the sea rough, the sky heavily overcast with a thin, miserable drizzle reducing visibility. The *Atlantis* was very close to the other ship before her lookouts sighted her.

Called to the bridge of the raider, Kapitän Rogge examined the dark outline of the ship through his binoculars. She had the appearance of a run-of-the-mill Allied merchantman, but she was acting in a most unorthodox manner. Far from making maximum speed and, perhaps, zig-zagging, as any unescorted ship would be expected to do in these waters, she was steaming at slow speed and stopping from time to time. Mindful of the fact that several British armed merchant cruisers were reported to be in the area, Rogge was suspicious. He altered course and steamed parallel to the stranger, matching her slow speed. The longer he observed her actions, the more he became convinced that she was a British AMC and, as such, posed a deadly threat to his ship.

It is an established fact that in the small hours of the morning the human mind is at its lowest ebb and liable to magnify the unexplained out of all proportions. It is possible that for this reason it did not then occur to Rogge that, had the other ship been an enemy warship, her lookouts would have been every bit as alert as his own and either a challenge or a broadside would have come his way long since. In the event the *Atlantis* continued to shadow her suspected adversary, waiting for the dawn.

Aboard the *King City* it had been one of those nights sent to try the patience of even the most equable of seamen. The miserable weather had coincided with the breakdown of one of the boiler-room fans, without which the ship could not raise sufficient steam to keep the main engine running smoothly. A night-long battle fought by her engineers had kept the British ship limping through the stormy darkness at reduced speed, sometimes stopping and drifting as each attempted repair came to naught. As dawn began to push back the shadows of the wheelhouse, the *King City*'s chief officer, who had the watch, became aware of the presence of another ship, close on the quarter, and seemingly keeping pace with them. He reached for the signal lamp, intending to flash a challenge.

At that precise moment Bernhard Rogge concluded that he was almost certainly in close contact with a British armed merchant cruiser, a not very alert one, but a ship he dare not allow to get in the first blow. At his signal, the *Atlantis* ran up her battle ensigns and opened fire with her 5.9s. The range was so short that it was impossible for the experienced German gunners to miss the slow-steaming ship. The first two shells exploded in the *King City*'s midships accommodation, killing instantly her four apprentices, her assistant cook and the deck boy, all of whom lay asleep in their bunks. Not one of them had lived to see his eighteenth birthday.

Within minutes of being hit the *King City* was ablaze from end to end, the gas generated by the 5000 tons of coal in her holds turning her into a gigantic, self-feeding inferno. It was very much to Rogge's credit that, as soon as he realized he had fired on a harmless cargo ship without warning, his first thought was to save what lives he could. The sea was rough and the swell running high, and no real blame could have been attached to the raider's captain if he had left the men of the *King City* to their fate. They were, after all, enemies. But Rogge was a humane man. He ordered his first lieutenant, Ulrich Mohr, to take the boats away.

Approaching the burning ship, Mohr was able to confirm Rogge's conclusion beyond doubt. She was indeed a far cry from being a British warship, her only visible armament being a single 4-inch on her stern, which was unmanned, its barrel pointing harmlessly at the sky. In no sense could this ship be said to present a threat to the *Atlantis*. However, the damage had been done.

As Mohr's two whalers came within 300 yards of the *King City*, the fierce heat of the flames could be felt and men were seen throwing themselves over the side. Others were struggling desperately to lower boats and launch rafts. Despite the heavy seas, Mohr brought his boats alongside the doomed ship and managed to rescue thirty-eight men from the flames, including some injured, who Captain Marshall refused to leave behind.

Although alight from stem to stern, the *King City* brought great credit to her British builders by stubbornly refusing to sink. Eventually Rogge, impatient to clear the area, was forced to close the range and expend more ammunition on the blazing wreck. When she did finally sink beneath the waves, the *King City* did so with an angry hissing of steam as the sea came in contact with her red-hot superstructure.

Once safe aboard the German raider, the survivors expressed their gratitude to Rogge and Mohr for their rescue, but also made plain their bitterness at what they saw as the unnecessary killing of the six young boys. To them it was as though the whole of the youth of their small ship-bound community had been wiped out for no good reason other than a suspicion that their ship might be a threat to the raider. The men of the *Atlantis*, Rogge in particular, would have it otherwise. While they genuinely regretted the deaths of the boys, they argued, understandably, that they could not afford to take risks. For the *Atlantis*, alone and far from home, one mistake might be one too many.

By the middle of October, with another string of merchant ships fallen under her guns, the *Atlantis* began to run into serious problems. In addition to her 347 crew, she now had on board over 300 prisoners. Food and water were running short and the accommodation available for prisoners was dangerously overcrowded. Fortunately, a solution came to hand on the 22nd of the month when a Yugoslav tramp was captured off the Sunda Strait. The 5000-ton, 28-year-old *Durmitor* – in her better days the British ship *Plutarch* – was a seedy, run-down ship, rusty, dirty and loaded with a full cargo of bulk salt. But to Berhard Rogge she was a means to an end. With an armed prize crew on board, and 240 ex-*Atlantis* prisoners penned in a barbed wire compound on her deck, the *Durmitor* set sail for the nearest Axis-held port, Mogadishu in Italian Somaliland.

The voyage turned out to be one of sheer misery for the Allied prisoners of war, among their number Captain Harry Marshall and his thirty-seven surviving crew from the *King City*. At night, and in bad weather, the only shelter the prisoners had was in the *Durmitor*'s two forward holds, on top of the cargo of bulk salt.

41

Here it was always cold and damp, and overrun with giant rats, of which the Yugoslav carried a veritable army. Sleep was impossible and to this was added hunger and thirst. The 3,400-mile passage across the Indian Ocean to Mogadishu should have taken the *Durmitor* about nineteen days at her average speed of 7½ knots, but her Yugoslav chief engineer, to cover up some previous malpractice, had produced a fictitious set of bunker figures. The ship did not, in fact, have anything like enough coal on board to reach Mogadishu. Inevitably, speed was reduced conserve fuel, so that the estimated nineteen days stretched out to twenty-nine, resulting in the prisoners suffering the additional privation of strict food and water rationing.

The *Durmitor*, having burned most of her cabin furniture and hatchboards in her boiler furnaces, finally fetched up near the small village of Uarsiech, 40 miles to the north of Modgadishu, on 20 November. The prisoners, many of them now in a very sorry state, were put into an Italian prisoner of war camp, where conditions were to prove, if anything, worse than on board the *Durmitor*. The men remained in the camp for four months, during which fever was rampant and four of their number died of dysentery.

When the *King City*'s men, all fortunately still alive, and their fellow prisoners were released from captivity by the Gold Coast Regiment in March 1941 they were sick, emaciated and mentally drained. Yet, while they had harsh things to say about their treatment at the hands of the Germans and Italians, they were bitterly disappointed and hurt at their reception by the British authorities in Somaliland. There seemed to be an excellent procedure for dealing with ex-POWs from the Armed Services, but the merchant seamen were treated like lepers and left to fend for themselves. This was a bitter pill for men to swallow who had lost their ships and suffered months of captivity and hardship.

Nine months after the *King City*'s survivors were set free, the *Atlantis* finally ran out of luck. On the morning of 21 November 1941, while she lay stopped north of the Kerguelen Islands refuelling *U-126*, she was spotted by a Walrus from the British cruiser *Devonshire*, commanded by Captain R.D. Oliver, which was patrolling in the area. *Devonshire* came racing in and the raider was soon under fire. A shell hit her main magazine and she blew up and sank, taking seven of her crew with her. The *Atlantis*, who in her short piratical career had sent twenty-two Allied merchantmen totalling 135,697 tons to the bottom, was no more.

The story did not end there for the survivors of the German raider. Wary of the intentions of *U-126*, which had dived when *Devonshire* came on the scene, Captain Oliver withdrew, leaving Rogge and his men to their fate. However, when the British cruiser was out of sight, the U-boat surfaced and her commander, Kapitänleutnant Ernst Bauer, took the *Atlantis'* boats in tow, handing them over two days later to the German supply ship *Python*. The survivors were still on board that ship when, on 1 December, she stopped to refuel two more U-boats, *U-A* and *U-68*. While she was thus engaged, over the horizon came the *Devonshire*'s twin sister, HMS *Dorsetshire*, and for the second time Rogge and his men found themselves taking to the boats from a ship on fire and sinking. Thereafter followed an amazing rescue operation, carried out by four U-boats, who crammed the 400 survivors into their hulls and transported them safely back to Germany. One of the rescue boats was the Italian submarine *Tazzoli*, commanded by Carlo Fecia di Cossato, of whom more later.

North Atlantic Massacre

The Canadian port of Three Rivers lies on the St Maurice River near to the point where it empties into the St Lawrence Estuary, almost 800 miles from the sea. In the war years Three Rivers was one of the main loading terminals for the vast quantities of steel and timber flowing from Canada across the Atlantic to a beleaguered Britain. In late September 1940 two of the berths in Three Rivers were occupied by the steamers *Beatus* and *Fiscus*, which comprised fifty per cent of the Tempus Shipping Company's fleet.

The Cardiff-based shipping company of Sir William Seager, otherwise Tempus Shipping, owned only four ships at the outbreak of the war. In outward appearance they were the usual run-of-the-mill tramps, distinguished only by their unusual names, *Amicus*, *Beatus*, *Fiscus* and *Salvus*. They were, however, known worldwide as being among the most efficient and best-kept ships sailing out of the Bristol Channel. The *Salvus* had already received her baptism of fire in the North Sea when she had successfully fought off an attack by German bombers earlier in the year. Her three sisters had so far eluded the enemy, which, thirteen months into a war that had to date claimed nearly 500 British merchant ships, must have been some considerable satisfaction to their owners and their crews. This equable state of affairs was about to be upset.

The *Beatus*, of 4,885 tons, commanded by Captain William Brett, and the *Fiscus*, also of 4855 tons, under the command of Captain Ebenezer Williams, were in adjacent berths in Three Rivers, taking on cargo for British ports. Neither ship was in the first bloom of her youth, the *Beatus* having been built in 1925, while the *Fiscus* was only five years her junior. However, in the tradition of Tempus Shipping, both ships were in first class condition and, in more normal times, would have been well fitted for the coming voyage across the North Atlantic.

Captain Brett of the *Beatus* was in good spirits as the loading of his ship neared completion. His cargo was a satisfying one, being full cubic and full deadweight, a state of loading rarely achieved. At the bottom of the lower holds of the *Beatus* was stowed a layer of heavy steel ingots, with the remaining space up to the hatch-tops packed with planks of Canadian timber. On deck, to a height of twelve feet, was stowed more timber. Not one cubic inch of space, nor one inch of freeboard had been wasted. Brett was comforted by the knowledge that, should his ship take a torpedo, her cargo of timber would keep her afloat for a considerable time. In the North Atlantic that could mean the difference between life and death for Brett and his crew.

On board the *Fiscus* Captain Ebenezer Williams was in a less happy frame of mind. The planners had seen fit to load his ship with a full deadweight cargo of steel ingots, topped off with a few crates of aircraft. In consequence, the *Fiscus* had too much weight too low down in her holds and was therefore guaranteed to roll her scuppers under all the way across the Atlantic. Furthermore, a single torpedo would send her to the bottom like a stone. It was this last possibility that weighed heavily on Williams' mind. He had survived the First World War at sea and, so far, this one, but he now had a strong premonition that the final reckoning would come soon. He had made known his fears to Brett, who had done his best to dispel them, but Williams would have none of it. He was convinced that neither he nor the *Fiscus* would see the other side of the Atlantic.

The two ships joined Convoy SC 7 at Sydney, Cape Breton, at the entrance to the Gulf of St Lawrence, on 4 October. It is doubtful if Brett and Williams took any heart at the sight of the thirty-three elderly ships they found assembled in the large and sheltered bay of Sydney harbour. They were not an inspiring bunch, the Convoy Commodore sailing in the 26-year-old *Assyrian*, a cargo vessel of less than 3000 tons, which would have been more at home in the Mediterranean than in the North Atlantic at the equinox. Someone – an experienced seaman he obviously was not – had also decided to send with this convoy the Great Lakes steamers *Eaglescliffe Hall*, *Trevisa* and *Winona*, each of only 1,800 tons gross and well past pensionable age. The other ships, half of them under the Red Ensign, could only be described as a motley collection of rusty geriatrics, all about to set sail into a hostile ocean dominated by a very powerful enemy.

SC 7 sailed out of Sydney, Cape Breton, on 5 October, led by the diminutive *Assyrian*, and escorted by the Canadian armed yacht *Elk* and the 1000-ton sloop HMS *Scarborough*, the latter hardly a sight to strike fear into the heart of the enemy, or, for that matter, to boost the confidence of those involved. On the credit side the weather was good, fine and clear with no more than a fresh breeze blowing. But the North Atlantic seldom rests easy for long and the first of the winter gales soon came sweeping in. On the 7th HMCS *Elk*, short of fuel and unable to withstand the heavy seas, turned back, leaving *Scarborough* as the sole escort. Four of the merchantmen, including the 1800-ton *Trevisa*, also fell out and were left to straggle along behind.

Fighting to hold ranks, the remainder of the convoy edged slowly eastwards, challenging the worsening weather for every mile gained. By the 16th, at the northernmost point of their route, and still unmolested by the enemy, hopes were running high. They were then only four days steaming from the northern approaches to the British Isles and the hard-pressed *Scarborough* had been joined by the sloop *Fowey* and the corvette *Bluebell*. It was then that they heard the plaintive calls for help from the little *Trevisa*, straggling astern. The U-boats had made their first kill. There was nothing for the other ships to do but to close ranks and wait for the coming onslaught. As if sensing the approaching drama, the wind fell away and the sea ceased its angry raging.

SC 7 did not have long to wait. Just before midnight on the 16th Kapitänleutnant Heinrich Bleichrodt in *U-48*, who had for some time been aimlessly scanning an empty ocean with his binoculars, sighted the slow-moving mass of ships. He immediately radioed Lorient for assistance and then began to stalk his prey. On the receipt of Bleichrodt's sighting report, Admiral

Dönitz ordered his North Atlantic force into action. In the area were Otto Kretschmer in *U-99*, Englebert Endrass in *U-46*, Fritz Frauenheim in *U-101*, Joachim Schepke in *U-100* and Karl-Heinz Moehle in *U-123*. Between them these ace commanders had already accounted for a total of seventy-eight Allied merchant ships. Now they raced to station themselves in a north-south line ahead of the convoy, setting up a lethal trap into which SC 7 must sail.

At 0500 on the 17th Heinrich Bleichrodt began his lone attack with a fan of torpedoes which sank the 3843-ton *Scoresby*, the French tanker *Languedoc* and damaged the 4678-ton *Haspenden*. But in attacking on the surface and so near to dawn, Bleichrodt made a mistake that almost proved fatal for *U-48*. A Sunderland flying boat of RAF Coastal Command, the first air cover for the convoy, spotted the marauding submarine and dived to attack. The Sunderland's bombs did no damage to *U-48*, but Bleichrodt was forced to go deep. If the U-boat had then been ignored – for she had suffered a severe shock and was unlikely to return to the attack – the tragedy that befell SC 7 in the next seventy-two hours might have been lessened. Unfortunately, *Scarborough* gave chase, spending most of that day hunting *U-48*. By the time the sloop broke off empty-handed, she was so far astern of the convoy that she was never able to rejoin.

In the early hours of the 18th SC 7 had acquired a new shad-ower in the form of *U-38*, commanded by Kapitänleutnant Heinrich Liebe, who had also come upon the ships by chance. After reporting the convoy's position to Dönitz, who in turn sent an up-date to his waiting wolf pack, Liebe made a rather half-hearted sortie, damaging only one ship, the 3670-ton Glasgow steamer *Carsbreck*. He then broke off the action. Shortly after Liebe had withdrawn on the morning of the 18th, the convoy escort was reinforced by the sloop HMS *Leith* and the corvette HMS *Heartsease*. The guard around SC 7 now consisted of two sloops and two corvettes, none of which unfortunately had any experience of operating with the others. It was therefore a some-what fragmented group. But as the convoy was now only 150 miles from the west coast of Ireland and well within the reach of air cover there were grounds for optimism. Then, at 1900 on the evening of the 18th, in fine, clear weather, SC 7 sailed into the German trap.

The least experienced of Dönitz's aces, Karl-Heinz Moehle, in *U-123*, opened the attack and all but bungled the whole thing. He fired at the 5458-ton British ship *Shekatika*, which was then romping ahead of the convoy, but failed to sink her. The more experienced Endrass, in *U-46*, then moved in quickly before the escorts could coordinate their defence.

The lookout on the bridge of the *Beatus* was first to sight *U-46*, as her low outline was briefly silhouetted by the moonlight on the port bow. His cry of warning alerted Captain Brett, who just had time to order the transmission of the submarine attack warning SSSS before the torpedo struck. Endrass had aimed well. The torpedo caught the *Beatus* squarely amidships on her port side, causing rapid flooding of the engine-room and adjacent holds. A brief inspection of the chaos below decks was enough to convince Brett that his ship was damaged beyond all salvation and would, despite her cargo of timber, soon sink. He gave the order to abandon ship.

As so often happens when abandoning ship at night under such horrific circumstances, there was a certain amount of confusion. One lifeboat was lost through a panicking Asian fireman cutting though the rope falls with an axe, but, fortunately, the boat was not yet manned and no lives were lost. The small jolly boat was pressed into service and Brett and his crew were able to get away from the sinking ship.

Following the torpedoing of the *Beatus*, the Convoy Commodore ordered the remaining ships to scatter. This was a mistake and the slaughter then began in earnest. With the corvette *Heartsease* having left to stand by the *Carsbreck*, damaged by *U-38*, and the *Scarborough* still some miles astern, the other escorts, two sloops and a corvette, could do little more than chase their own tails, while the U-boats, manoeuvring on the surface with impunity, moved in for the kill. In the following two and a half hours five more merchantmen were sunk and the *Shekatika* again damaged.

When the first fury of the battle had died down the 2118-ton

Dutch ship *Boekolo*, commanded by Captain J. de Groot, decided to return to the convoy and in doing so came upon the two boats containing Captain William Brett and the twenty-seven men of the *Beatus*, which, in spite of her cargo of timber, had taken only forty minutes to go down. Making a brave, but in retrospect foolish, decision, Captain de Groot stopped his ship and made ready to pick up the survivors. The first boat was alongside the *Boekolo* when Joachim Schepke in *U-100* appeared on the scene and without hesitation put an end to de Groot's mission of mercy. Schepke's torpedo took the *Boekolo* in her No.4 hold and, taking a heavy list to port, she began to go down by the stern. *Beatus*' messboy, who had been the only survivor to reach the deck of the *Boekolo*, joined the Dutchmen in their boats.

Horrified by the unopposed destruction going on around him, and still filled with the sense of foreboding that had been with him since before sailing from Three Rivers, Captain Ebenezer Williams pulled the heavily-laden *Fiscus* out of the convoy and rang for full revolutions. Under the circumstances prevailing, his decision to make a run for it could not be challenged, for the tiny escort force of SC 7 was now completely overwhelmed. However, Williams had made his move too late. The wily Otto Kretschmer was already closing in for his twenty-fifth kill of the war.

U-99's torpedo ripped open the hull plates of the *Fiscus*, and with all her reserve buoyancy cancelled out by the great weight of steel in her holds, she plunged to the bottom like a stone. Ebenezer Williams and his 27-man crew, which included two boys of fourteen and fifteen, went with her.

The battle, if such a one-sided conflict could be so called, continued throughout the night of the 18th and into the early hours of the next day. Only when, at around 0400 on the 19th, the U-boats had expended all their torpedoes did they break off and fade away into the coming dawn. By this time Convoy SC 7 had lost twenty-one ships out of the thirty-five that had set sail from Cape Breton fourteen days earlier. Two more were badly damaged. Captain Brett and the men of the *Beatus* were picked up by the corvette *Bluebell*, while the survivors of the *Boekolo*, including the *Beatus'* messboy, found safety in the sloop *Fowey*. All were landed at Gourock on the 20th.

The destruction of SC 7 was the first big action of the battle of the Atlantic and should have been a salutary warning to the British Admiralty. To send convoys of small, slow and lightly escorted merchant ships across a North Atlantic seething with U-boats was folly enough in summer; in winter, as with SC 7, it was little short of ritual murder for the merchant seamen involved. Unfortunately, the lesson never really sank home.

As to those who, in this winter of 1940 massacred SC 7, Englebert Endrass was to lose his life in *U-567* when she was destroyed by the sloop HMS *Deptford* off the west coast of Spain in December 1941. *U-46* faded into obscurity and was scuttled in May 1945. Otto Kretschmer, the ace of all U-boat aces, was at large until March 1941, when, in *U-99*, he was caught by the destroyer HMS *Walker* while attacking Convoy HX 112 in the North Atlantic. *U-99* was sunk, but most of her crew, including Kretschmer, were taken prisoner.

Long Odds

In the early winter of 1940, for the first time since Napoleon Bonaparte massed his invasion barges in the Channel ports, Britain faced a serious threat of invasion. A decisive battle had been won in the air, but Hitler's victorious army was still poised, awaiting the opportunity to cross the English Moat. The whole emphasis of British air and sea reconnaissance was therefore now concentrated on the Channel and the Southern North Sea. The time was ideal for the German pocket battleship *Admiral Scheer* to break out into the Atlantic.

Launched in 1933, and only ready for service after the outbreak of war, the 10,000-ton *Admiral Scheer* carried, in addition to torpedoes and anti-aircraft guns, six 11-inch and eight 5.9-inch guns. She had a top speed of 26½ knots and a range of 19,000 miles without refuelling. Commanded by Kapitän-zur-See Theodor Krancke, she left the Baltic on 23 October 1940 and reached the Atlantic via the Denmark Strait undetected by British patrols. Krancke had orders to mount an attack on British convoys, many of which were now only very lightly defended due to the withdrawal of Royal Navy ships to the Mediterranean following the Italian declaration of war.

In late October 1940 the 4955-ton *Fresno City*, registered in Bideford and owned by the Reardon Smith Line, lay at anchor at Sydney, Cape Breton, loaded to her Winter North Atlantic marks with 8,129 tons of Canadian maize. She was to form part of one of the largest and fastest convoys ever to cross the Atlantic from west to east. Although not enamoured with the prospect of a winter crossing, the *Fresno City*'s master, Captain

R.L. Lawson, had every confidence in his ship, which was well-found in all respects, had a sea speed of 14 knots and carried the standard merchant ship armament of 4-inch and 12-pounder guns.

The rest of the assembled convoy, viewed through Lawson's binoculars, presented a brave sight. They were smart looking ships, all of them, and included the New Zealand Shipping Company's 16,698-ton *Rangitiki*, and several large tankers. The Commodore's ship was the *Fresno City*'s 4-year-old sister ship *Cornish City*, under the command of Captain John O'Neill. Lawson's mood of optimism faded when he swung his binoculars on to Convoy HX 84's sole escort vessel. She was the 14,164-ton armed merchant cruiser *Jervis Bay*, an ex-Aberdeen & Commonwealth liner. Built in 1922, the AMC was armed with seven 5.9-inch guns, which were even older than herself, and had a top speed of only 15 knots. She was a sad reflection on Britain's naval strength at this stage of the war.

Convoy HX 84 sailed from Sydney on the evening of 27 October 1940, at about the same time as the *Admiral Scheer* was leaving the Kiel Canal at Brunsbüttel to make her stealthy way north to the Denmark Strait. The *Fresno City* was comfortably stationed in the middle of the convoy, immediately astern of the *Jervis Bay*. Steering an east-south-easterly course, the ships made for a prearranged rendezvous in 41°N 43°W, where at first light on 2 November they were joined by ships homeward bound from ports south of the Chesapeake River and Canada's west coast. The merger resulted in a convoy of thirty-eight ships carrying over a quarter of a million tons of vital cargo for British ports. There was no increase in the convoy's escort force commensurate with its expansion. Forming up into nine columns abreast, and covering some 10 square miles of ocean, HX 84 set a north-easterly course for the north-western approaches to the British Isles.

At the same time, 450 miles to the south-west of HX 84, the British refrigerated vessel *Mopan*, homeward bound from Jamaica with 70,000 stems of bananas, was heading north-eastwards at high speed. The *Mopan* crossed ahead and in sight of HX 84 on the forenoon of the 5th, but did not exchange signals.

The weather at the time was fine, with excellent visibility, and the *Mopan*'s crew no doubt felt a thrill of pride as their ship raced across ahead of the convoy. They were unaware that 50 miles or so to the north-east the *Admiral Scheer* was searching for HX 84, which Krancke had been advised was somewhere in the area. A little after 1300 that day the *Mopan* sailed into his arms, and Krancke stopped her with a couple of well-aimed shells.

The first reaction of the *Mopan*'s captain when his ship came under fire was to send a message warning HX 84 of the enemy's presence, but he was forestalled in this by Krancke, who threatened to blow the *Mopan* out of the water if she used her radio. By 1600, having been abandoned by her crew in good order, the British fruit-carrier was a burning wreck. Had she been able to send out the customary RRRR (I am being attacked by a surface raider) signal, HX 84 would have gained a small advantage that might have saved many lives, but it would not have escaped the *Admiral Scheer*, whose Arado reconnaissance plane had already sighted the smoke of the convoy.

Oblivious to the danger it was running into, HX 84 continued to steam steadily to the north-east until, at 1540, the *Rangitiki* signalled the Commodore in the *Cornish City* reporting smoke at four points on her port bow. At 1700 the *Empire Penguin* reported a ship approaching the convoy from a northerly direction. HX 84 was then in position 53° 50' N 32° 15' W, about halfway between Newfoundland and Ireland. Six minutes later the *Fresno City*'s chief officer sighted what appeared to be a warship on the port beam. He called Captain Lawson to the bridge. As he hurried up the bridge ladder Lawson heard the Commodore's sound signal ordering an emergency turn to starboard and reached the bridge just in time to see the first salvo from the *Admiral Scheer*'s 11-inch guns straddle the *Jervis Bay*. The AMC was in the centre of the convoy, midway between the 4th and 5th columns, and while, she was untouched, one shell demolished the forward funnel of the *Rangitiki*, leading Column 6, and another hit the *Cornish City*, leader of Column 5.

Lawson rang for emergency full speed and, with her engines working up to 14 knots and her helm hard to starboard, the

Fresno City followed the other ships in presenting her stern to the enemy. Their only defence was to make a run for it.

As the *Fresno City* heeled and slewed to starboard, Lawson watched with horror and admiration as the *Jervis Bay*, her guns firing, pulled out of the convoy and headed at full speed towards the *Admiral Scheer*. Captain E.S. Fogarty Fegen, the AMC's commander, his ship hopelessly outclassed in everything but the courage of himself and his crew, had no intention of allowing the convoy to be savaged.

The fight was cruelly one-sided, and soon over. Before the *Jervis Bay* could bring her ancient 5.9s within range of the enemy, Lawson saw her hit on her port side, where fire broke out immediately. The next 11-inch salvo all but demolished the bridge of the unarmoured ex-passenger liner, starting further fires. Lawson shook his head sadly and turned away. He must look to his own ship.

The *Fresno City*'s gun's crew was already closed up at her 4-inch stern gun and, more in the way of a gesture of defiance than anything else, Lawson gave the order to open fire on the raider. Other ships in the convoy did the same, but the range was too great, the *Admiral Scheer* being 6 or 7 miles astern. Smoke floats were dropped by the fleeing ships in an effort to cover their escape, but these proved ineffective.

The *Jervis Bay* was by now stopped and burning furiously, her guns silent, but she had achieved what Captain Fogarty Fegen set out to do; the merchant ships were scattered and steaming away from the enemy at maximum speed. Thanks to the sacrifice of Fogarty Fegen and his men, the unopposed massacre Krancke had looked for was not to be. Aboard the *Fresno City*, Lawson, keeping a close eye of the *Admiral Scheer*, brought the ship round onto a course of 270° and steamed west into the gathering twilight. Once under the cover of darkness, he intended gradually to assume a south-westerly course in the hope of slipping around the stern of the raider.

The *Jervis Bay*, ablaze from stem to stern, her hull holed below the waterline and her steering gear smashed, finally sank three hours later. Captain Fogarty Fegen and 185 of his crew went down with her. The outcome of their fight had been wholly predictable. An elderly merchant ship, armed only with 5.9-inch guns left over from the 19th century, was no match for a modern pocket battleship with 11-inch guns. Valiantly though she tried, she had simply not been able to bring her guns into range of the *Admiral Scheer* before she was reduced to a burning hulk, but she had given the merchant ships a chance to survive. Every one of her crew would have died had it not been for the Swedish cargo ship *Stûreholm* which, in an outstanding display of courage and compassion, slipped back under the guns of the *Admiral Scheer* and snatched sixty-eight men from the water. Three of these were dead when picked up.

Meanwhile, the *Fresno City*, having only the 9800-ton London-registered *Beaverford* in company, was making good progress to the south. The two ships were on slightly divergent courses, so that the distance between them was gradually opening. Astern, Captain Lawson could still see the flames from the other ships caught by the German raider's guns, but, for the time being at least, it seemed that his ship and the *Beaverford* had got away. Then, at 2150, more than four hours after the convoy had scattered, the *Beaverford*, which was about 10 miles off the *Fresno City*'s port beam, suddenly came under fire and burst into flames.

Unable to see the enemy, Lawson altered course away from the *Beaverford* and, for the second time that night, rang for emergency full speed. His engineers responded again and, with her pistons hammering out a mad tattoo, and her hull shaking like a thing possessed, the *Fresno City* fled into the night. After about fifty minutes of frenzied steaming she seemed to be completely alone on the ocean and Lawson breathed a cautious sigh of relief.

But it was short-lived, for at that moment, from a shadowy form unseen on the starboard quarter, a searchlight snapped on, and the *Fresno City* was bathed in brilliant light. Moving with the speed and stealth of a stalking leopard, the *Admiral Scheer* had caught up with the fleeing merchantman and was about to pounce.

The range was point-blank – no more than 200 yards Lawson judged – so the killing was swift and precise. In rapid succession, seven shells crashed into the *Fresno City*, two finding a target in her engine-room, then one in each of her holds, working from forward to aft. Her engine, which had been labouring magnificently, came to a sudden stop. From her holds hatchboards, tarpaulins and beams were hurled high into the air and flames leapt from the open hatches as her cargo of grain ignited and began to burn fiercely. Lawson, who was in the starboard wing of the bridge and still blinded by the *Admiral Scheer*'s searchlight, came near to death when a heavy object – possibly a steel hatch beam – crashed down onto the bridge. Half-stunned, he lunged for the button of the air whistle to sound the alarm. The whistle gave no response, for the air lines had been cut in the bombardment.

There was little to be done for the *Fresno City* now. Lawson sent his chief officer below to muster all hands to the boats by word of mouth, then he stood by on the bridge until the way was off the ship. This took about five minutes, after which Lawson went to the boat deck to supervise the abandoning of the ship. To his great surprise, he found the deck deserted, with the port lifeboat gone, and the starboard boat upended and hanging from one fall, its bow only a few feet above the water and in danger of being smashed against the ship's side by the heavy swell.

As there was nothing Lawson could do with the boat on his own, he went in search of help. He found the engine-room ablaze and empty of life, the after accommodation yielding the same negative result. Moving back amidships, he met up with Second Officer Gleghorn and nine other men, who had been sheltering from shrapnel in the saloon alleyway. Sending them to secure the starboard lifeboat, Lawson went forward where he discovered absolute carnage. The shell fired by the *Admiral Scheer* into the forward hold had exploded in the vacant space above the cargo, completely wrecking and setting fire to the crews' accommodation under the forecastle head. Ordinary Seaman Douglas Smith lay dead and two able seamen, Mackie and Finnis were seriously injured. The deck boy, W.H. Lynn, who had been on lookout on the forecastle head, was missing.

Under the direction of Second Officer Gleghorn, the starboard lifeboat was lowered to the water and made secure. The injured were brought aft and, with great difficulty owing to the swell, lowered into the boat. Only then was the *Fresno City* finally abandoned. The time was 2130, exactly half an hour after the *Admiral Scheer*'s first shell had struck home. Captain Lawson was last to leave the ship, after which the boat was pulled clear, fighting for every inch gained against the wind and sea, which were threatening to smash it against the ship's side. Once out of danger, Lawson's next thought was for the other lifeboat, which he hoped contained the rest of his crew. Within a few minutes the boat was sighted some way off to port lying to a sea anchor, but it was another two hours before the two boats were brought together. Lawson then streamed the sea anchor of his boat and for the next three hours the boats lay hove to and rising and falling on the swell while their mother ship continued to burn. Shortly after 0200 on 6 November Lawson's sea anchor carried away, and the boats drifted apart, never again to regain contact.

By 0400 the *Fresno City* was almost completely burned out. Then the flames began to subside and, for a while, she was visible only as a dark silhouette against the night sky. At 0435 by Lawson's watch the whole superstructure of the ship was seen to fall in on itself and the *Fresno City* slowly slipped beneath the waves.

Now that all hope of reboarding the ship had gone Lawson made the two injured men as comfortable as possible, hoisted the boat's sails and shaped a course for the position where the convoy was first attacked – some 80 miles away, he calculated. There he hoped a ship, or ships, might by now be searching for survivors of the previous night's disaster. But when they finally reached that position, at noon on the 7th, the sea was empty as far as the eye could see. There was nothing else for it but to sail eastwards where, 900 miles or so away, lay the coast of Ireland.

A westerly gale blew up on the 8th, bringing with it a rough, tumbling sea, but Lawson's boat behaved well, running before the wind under a jib sail only. Shortly after dawn on the 9th smoke was sighted on the horizon to the south-east and Lawson immediately altered course towards it. Soon the mast and funnel of a merchant ship were visible. A few hours later Lawson and his men were picked up by the Greek ship *Mount Taygetus*. They had sailed 200 miles from the scene of the sinking of the *Fresno City*. Once aboard the Greek vessel, which was commanded by Captain Samathrakis, the British survivors were treated with the utmost warmth and hospitality, the injured men receiving particular attention.

The *Fresno City*'s second lifeboat was also eventually found and with all on board safe. Despite the destruction caused by the *Admiral Scheer*'s 11-inch shells and the subsequent confused abandonment of the ship, Lawson had lost only one man. The rest of HX 84 had also fared better than might have been expected. Due mainly to the heroic actions of Captain Fogarty Fegen and the men of the armed merchant cruiser *Jervis Bay*, the convoy had been able to scatter effectively, with the result that the German raider, for all her speed and big guns, succeeded in sinking only four merchant ships other than the *Fresno City*. The British tanker *San Demetrio*, loaded with 7000 tons of gasoline, was set on fire and abandoned, but she was later reboarded by some of her crew and reached port with most of her precious cargo intact. Three days after the *Admiral Scheer* attacked, the 2374-ton Swedish ship *Vingaland* was bombed by a Focke-Wulf and finally sunk by the Italian submarine *Marconi*. In all, thirty-one of the thirty-eight ships sailing with Convoy HX 84 reached port safely, but the loss of life in the action was heavy, 206 merchant seamen and 186 men of the Royal Navy having perished.

The *Admiral Scheer* was to sink another nine Allied merchantmen in the South Atlantic before returning to Kiel in April 1941. Thereafter, as a result of Hitler's increasing reluctance to risk his big ships, she did little more than skulk in the Norwegian fjords, posing a threat to the convoys to North Russia. In 1944 she was destroyed by Allied bombers while in drydock at Kiel.

1. SS *Lanarth*, sunk in the Western Approaches by *U-30* 28 June 1940
(Welsh Industrial & Maritime Museum).

2. SS *King City* on fire and sinking in the Indian Ocean after attack by the German raider *Atlantis* on 24 August 1940 *(Reardon Smith Line).*

3. SS *Fiscus*, sunk by *U-99* in the North Atlantic 18 October 1940 *(A. Duncan)*.

4. SS *Beatus*, sunk by *U-46* in the North Atlantic 18 October 1940 *(A. Duncan)*.

5. MV *Fresno City*, sunk by the German pocket battleship *Admiral Scheer* in the North Atlantic 5 November 1940   *(Reardon Smith Line)*.

6. MV *Lady Glanely*, torpedoed by *U-101* and lost with all hands 400 miles west of Bloody Foreland 2 December 1940   *(Harold Appleyard)*.

7. SS *Sarastone* fought and won a gun duel with the Italian submarine *Mocenigo* off the west coast of Spain 22 December 1940 *(Welsh Industrial & Maritime Museum)*.

8. SS *Grelrosa*, bombed and sunk by a Focke-Wulf Condor 400 miles west of Malin Head 28 January 1941 *(Welsh Industrial & Maritime Museum)*.

9. SS *Garlinge*, sunk by *U-81* in the Mediterranean 10 November 1942 while taking part in the Allied invasion of North Africa *(Welsh Industrial & Maritime Museum)*.

10. SS *Llanashe*, sunk by *U-182* off South Africa 17 February 1943
(Welsh Industrial & Maritime Museum).

11. The *St Patrick* passing Strumble Head inbound to Fishguard.

12. MV *Cornish City*, sunk by *U-177* off Madagascar 29 July 1943
(Reardon Smith Line).

13. Winter in the North Atlantic. A corvette picking up survivors from a torpedoed merchant ship *(from a painting by Jack Sullivan)*.

14. Volunteer merchant gunners being introduced to a 12-pounder mounted on the poop deck *(Haven Puxley)*.

15. 88mm deck gun in action on a Type VII-C U-boat. It also carried one 37mm and two 20mm cannons *(Bundesarchiv)*.

16. Kapitänleutnant Ernst Mengersen in the conning tower of *U-101* *(Bundesarchiv)*.

17. A Type VII-C U-boat entering harbour *(Bundesarchiv)*.

9

The Wolves Gather

Meteorological Office statistics record the winter of 1940 as one of the worst winters in living memory in the North Atlantic. Those who sail this ocean on a regular basis would argue that winter in the North Atlantic is always a bad experience. It is so often one long, weary succession of depressions which, forming off Cape Hatteras, sweep across the great expanse of open water from west to east. These depressions are not merely local phenomena, but huge areas of low pressure up to 1000 miles across, and with central pressures as low as 960 millibars. In mid-Atlantic, where the systems reach the climax of their power, winds blow up to 100 knots, the swell is long and mountainous, with waves sometimes reaching over fifty feet high, before they topple over to fill the air with driving, salt-laden spray. Marching in company with the wind and waves comes the rain – thick, blanketing drizzle at first, turning to torrential rain, then spasmodic, stinging showers, cold and demoralizing. The North Atlantic winter is a miserable time.

In that winter of 1940 British and Allied merchant ships had much more to face than the familiar malevolence of the weather. The German U-boats were in full cry, organized by Admiral Dönitz into 'wolf packs', each with its own hunting ground. When the existence of a convoy had been established by Lorient, the word was flashed to the nearest wolf pack, which then fanned out and attempted to make contact. The first U-boat to sight the convoy became a shadow to the unsuspecting merchant ships, homing the rest of the pack in by radio. The concerted attack was usually made at night, with the U-boats working on the surface, where their speed often exceeded that of the convoy escorts. The result was all too often a dreadful blood-letting.

With the fall of France and the opening up of the Biscay coast to the U-boats, their numbers in the Atlantic increased dramatically. At the same time the Royal Navy was stretched by the Italian intervention in the war and there was an inevitable shortage of escorts for the Atlantic convoys. For many of the east-bound convoys – ships loaded with vital war supplies – the best they could expect for the greater part of the passage was the doubtful protection of an armed merchant cruiser. At a point about 600 miles to the west of Ireland a change-over of escorts with a west-bound convoy usually took place, the AMC handing over to the destroyer and corvette escort group which had guarded the outward-bound convoy thus far. In theory the east-bound ships then had maximum protection through the dangerous waters of the western approaches to the British Isles. Of course, under the conditions prevailing in winter, the interchange of escorts was anything but precise, one or both convoys being left unprotected for a number of hours. If Southern Ireland had been willing to allow Britain the use of air bases on her west coast, the change-over could have been covered by aircraft. However, although eagerly accepting goods brought across the Atlantic by British ships, the Irish were, in the words of Winston Churchill, 'quite content to sit happy and see us strangled'. At the same time there was evidence that German U-boats often used Irish harbours to shelter and refuel. Such was the situation in the North Atlantic when the 5497-ton motor-ship *Lady Glanely*, owned W.J. Tatem Ltd. and commanded by Captain Alexander Hughson, left Vancouver in early November 1940. She was deep-loaded with a general cargo topped off by timber on deck.

The 4000-mile passage from Vancouver to Balboa, at the Pacific end of the Panama Canal, was a peaceful twelve-day transfer from the cold Canadian winter to the sub-equatorial warmth of Panama Bay – no U-boats, no marauding aircraft. After much of one day spent negotiating the locks of the 42-mile-long canal, the *Lady Glanely* emerged into the deep blue of the Caribbean Sea, into an ocean paradise of hot days and warm nights. It seemed so far removed from the hell of a North Atlantic winter that no man on board, except perhaps Captain Hughson and his senior officers, could believe that that other world not only existed but was relentlessly drawing them into its dark and frightening void.

Threading her way through the islands of the West Indies, the *Lady Glanely* entered the Atlantic and headed north-westwards to Bermuda, where Convoy BHX 90 was assembling. BHX 90 sailed from Bermuda on 19 November and, four days later, in position 41°N 43°W, some 500 miles south-east Newfoundland, merged with a convoy out of Halifax, Nova Scotia. The enlarged convoy, designated HX 90, consisted of forty ships steaming in nine columns abreast, with the Commodore in the 5848-ton *Botavon*, commanded by Captain Henry Issac. The vice-commodore was in the 4739-ton *Victoria City*. Incredibly, in view of recent events, HX 90 was escorted by only one armed merchant cruiser, namely HMS *Laconia*.

The 19,695-ton ex-Cunard ship *Laconia* was one of the fifty passenger liners recruited into the Royal Navy early in the war to act as convoy escorts, thereby releasing the Navy's fighting ships for more offensive roles. This expedient strategy was doomed from the start. The AMCs were too slow, too cumbersome, possessed no protective armour plating and mounted mainly obsolete guns taken from scrapped warships. Already two of their number, the *Rawalpindi* and the *Jervis Bay* had found themselves matched against German capital ships and proved hopelessly outclassed on all counts, except the supreme courage and self-sacrifice of their commanders and crews. But bravery alone does not win battles. When confronted by determined U-boat attacks, the AMCs were even more vulnerable. Without Asdic or depth charges, they were not only useless in the defence of a convoy, but were defenceless themselves. Before they were withdrawn from service in 1942 fifteen of these expensive and heavily manned vessels had been sunk.

Shortly after the *Lady Glanely* and the other Bermuda ships joined up with HX 90 the first of the Atlantic storms moved in and for forty-eight hours the convoy was battered by high winds and heavy seas. Close station-keeping was impossible, most of

61

the heavily loaded ships hard pressed to do more than maintain steerage way. One by one, the less able, including the vice-commodore's ship *Victoria City*, dropped out, until, by the morning of the 26th, when the storm was subsiding, nine ships were missing. As there were no fast escorts available to round up the stragglers, the convoy re-formed as best it could and pressed on to the eastwards. The *Lady Glanely* was ordered by the Commodore to take up position as leader of the port column.

Even before HX 90 sailed from Halifax, the Admiralty had evidence to suggest that the route of the convoy had been leaked to the Germans by sources in Canada. It can, perhaps, be understood why this knowledge was withheld from the merchant ships, but there can be no conceivable excuse for not changing the route after sailing. This was not done, and the consequences were dire, for Admiral Dönitz had some of his best men at sea.

While HX 90 was reeling under the storm of 24/26 November, a thousand miles to the east the alerted U-boats were setting up an ambush. Forming up in an extended north-south line in the path of the convoy were the top-scoring ace Otto Kretschmer in *U-99*, Günther Prien, idol of the German public, in *U-47*, Herbert Kuppisch in *U-94*, Otto Salman in *U-52*, Gerd Schreiber in *U-95*, Hans-Peter Hinsch in *U-140*, Wolfgang Lüth in *U-43* and young Ernst Mengersen in *U-101*. Weather conditions for the projected ambush were almost perfect, with a force 4 to 6 wind giving waves high enough to make the trimmed-down boats difficult to see, while not seriously impeding their progress. Furthermore, visibility after dark was excellent, bright moonlight until about 2000, and brilliant Northern Lights throughout the night. Unknown to the U-boat commanders – or perhaps it was – they were to be handed yet another great advantage.

In accordance with current Admiralty practice, HX 90 was due to exchange escorts with the west-bound convoy OB 251 on the morning of 2 December in longitude 17 degrees west, or 250 miles west of Ireland. HMS *Laconia* was to return westwards with OB 251, while the destroyers *Vanquisher* and *Viscount*, the sloop *Folkestone* and the corvette *Gentian* would leave OB 251 and take over the shepherding of HX 90 to British waters. As the two convoys were routed to pass on parallel and opposite courses at about 90 miles apart, the change-over of escorts could not be simultaneous, but it was hoped the gap would be minimal. At best, this was an arrangement fraught with danger; in the event, it turned out to be a disaster for HX 90.

At 0700 on the morning of 1 December, with HX 90 maintaining steady progress to the east at 9½ knots, the Belgian ship *Ville D'Arlon* developed steering gear trouble and dropped out of the convoy. This was a common enough occurrence in any convoy, but on this occasion the straggling of the Belgian ship in daylight was to set in motion a tragic and bloody train of events.

Throughout the previous night Kapitänleutnant Ernst Mengersen, in *U-101*, had been scouting ahead of the wolf pack, but had made no sighting of the convoy, which was actually to the south of his search area. After dawn on the 1st Mengersen decided to try his luck to the south-east and in doing so completely missed HX 90. The convoy had already crossed ahead of him and was out of sight over the horizon by the time he reached its latitude. Unfortunately for HX 90 – and providentially for Mengersen – in the afternoon he came up with the *Ville D'Arlon*, which was again under way and steaming after the convoy at full speed. Mengersen tucked his boat in behind the Belgian ship and sent a sighting report to the rest of the pack.

The *Ville D'Arlon*, with *U-101* in close attendance, rejoined HX 90 at 1700 on the 1st at the same time as the *Laconia* said her farewells and left to join Convoy OB 251. The weather was fine, with the wind blowing west-south-west force 6, and darkness was drawing in. HX 90 was now steaming on an east-north-easterly course at 9½ knots, without escort and without any naval control, other than that exercised by the Commodore in the *Botavon*. The opportunity was too good to miss and Mengersen carefully manoeuvred *U-101* into position on the starboard side of the convoy and waited for the moon to set. At 2015 he fired a fan of three torpedoes, hitting first the 8826-ton British tanker *Appalachee* and one minute later the 4958-ton *Loch Ranza*. The third torpedo missed.

The convoy was now less than 300 miles to the west of Ireland and heavy rain had begun to fall. The explosions of Mengersen's torpedoes were heard on the bridge of the *Botavon* and confused lights seen in the direction of the starboard wing of the convoy, some 3 miles off, but no SOS messages were picked up or distress rockets seen. The Commodore, who had not been on the bridge at the time of the explosions, wrongly concluded that the sounds heard were thunder and the lights were signals between ships which had come near to colliding in the rain. He took no action.

Out on the starboard wing of the convoy, the *Appalachee* was sinking, while the *Loch Ranza*, herself damaged, was picking up survivors from the tanker. Both ships fell back into the darkness as the convoy continued on its unsuspecting way. Mengersen, who may not have been aware that HX 90 was now completely unescorted, had withdrawn to a safe distance, but was still in contact with the convoy.

At 0100 on the 2nd, HX 90 altered course to approach the pre-arranged rendezvous with the escorts coming from OB 251. Thirty minutes later the *Ville D'Arlon* again experienced a steering gear fault and once more prepared to drop astern. In doing so, she hoisted the customary 'not under command' signal of two red lights in a vertical line. However, these lights were not dimmed, as they should have been in wartime, and were in fact so bright that they could be seen by every ship in the convoy. If any of the U-boat wolf pack, called in by Mengersen, had any doubts about the position of the convoy, they were soon dispelled by the *Ville D'Arlon*'s lights. At 0210 Günther Prien, in *U-47*, put a torpedo into the Belgian ship and she sank quickly, taking with her the brilliant marker lights and, unfortunately, all her crew. But the damage had been done. The position of the unprotected HX 90 had been revealed to all and the wolf pack was moving in for the kill.

A massacre followed. The U-boats, unrestrained by the danger of retaliation, their helpless targets now illuminated by the Northern Lights, slipped in among the slow-moving columns of merchantmen and ranged up and down on the surface, torpedoing at will and using their deck guns when their tubes were empty. The convoy's only defence lay in a series of emergency turns, by which it was hoped to spoil the enemy's aim. Captain Issac, of the Commodore's ship *Botavon*, was later to say: 'I could not keep track of all the emergency turns as sometimes we had barely finished one when we had to go off again. We were like a helpless flock of sheep in a narrow lane with a dog on each side.'

In hindsight, it might have been wiser for the unescorted convoy to scatter at the first sign of a concerted attack, rather than stay bunched together sharing each other's agony. Most certainly Captain Alexander Hughson, in the *Lady Glanely*, would have been well advised to break away on his own. He commanded a powerful motorship, only two years old, and under pressure she would have been capable of 15 knots, perhaps more. But the discipline of the convoy, instilled into the merchant captains by dogmatic naval theorists over two years of war, was too great. Hughson continued to hold position as leader of the port wing column, with his engine ticking over at little more than half speed.

Just after 0300 Ernst Mengersen, having reloaded his tubes, positioned *U-101* abreast of the leading ships on the port side of the convoy. At 0320 the *Lady Glanely* moved into his sights and he fired. The torpedo hit the British ship squarely amidships. Eight minutes later Captain Hughson ordered his wireless operator to transmit the SSSS signal and then fired white distress rockets from the wing of the bridge. Mengersen, still on the surface, and able to aim and fire at his leisure, now torpedoed the 8376-ton tanker *Conch*, next ship astern of the *Lady Glanely*. Then he turned his sights on the 3862-ton steamer *Dunsley*, last ship in the column.

On the bridge of the *Dunsley*, her master, Captain J. Braithwaite, had heard the explosion ahead and seen the rockets arc up from the stricken *Lady Glanely*. He immediately altered course hard to starboard and, in doing so, avoided Mengersen's third torpedo. Braithwaite then made a very brave and humane decision, one which was contrary to the convoy rules, but in true Nelsonian tradition. Ignoring the obvious presence of the U-boats, he steamed at full speed for the position of the *Lady Glanely*, hoping that he might be able to snatch some survivors from the water. At 0350 the lifeboats of the *Lady Glanely*, which had by then sunk, were sighted and Braithwaite rang for slow speed. Twenty minutes later, the *Dunsley* was approaching the boats with boarding nets over the side, ready to pick up survivors. Her efforts came to naught, for at this point *U-47* intervened.

Braithwaite, occupied in manoeuvring his ship close to the *Lady Glanely*'s lifeboats, was informed of the sighting of the U-boat. She was on the surface half a mile off the *Dunsley*'s port beam and was clearly visible in the flare of the Northern Lights. Prien opened fire with his 88mm deck gun and Braithwaite, not a man to be intimidated, ordered his 4-inch gun's crew to return the fire. The fight was predictably one-sided. Although the *Dunsley*'s gunners claimed a hit on the U-boat, the ship was hit five times and caught fire. Reluctant though he was to leave the *Lady Glanely*'s lifeboats, Braithewaite's first duty was to his own crew. He aborted the rescue mission and, presenting his stern to *U-47*, he steamed away at full speed, zig-zagging to avoid the shells still bursting around him.

With the attack on the convoy rising to a fierce crescendo, there could be no more help for the men of the *Lady Glanely*. When the destroyer *Viscount* and a Sunderland flying boat searched the area on the morning of the 3rd the lifeboats had disappeared. No one, it seems, will ever know what happened to those thirty-one merchant seamen on that terrible winter's night in the North Atlantic.

The destruction of Convoy HX 90 continued. At 0515 the Liverpool-registered steamer *Kavak* was torpedoed and blew up. Seconds later the 1586-ton *Tasso* was also sunk, while the *Goodleigh*, sister ship to the *Lady Glanely*, was the victim of a savage attack by two U-boats. Günther Prien, who had sealed the fate of the survivors of the *Lady Glanely* by opening fire on the *Dunsley*, fired the first torpedo at the *Goodleigh*. She was hit on her starboard side directly under her bridge, which was partly destroyed by the explosion. With his ship settling ominously, Captain Quaite, who was injured, gave the order to take to the boats. While this operation was in progress, Otto Kretschmer, in *U-99*, approached the crippled ship and added three more torpedoes, the last of which caused the *Goodleigh*'s 4-inch magazine to explode. But the British ship had a full load of timber on board and despite her terrible wounds, she remained afloat for for several hours, allowing all her crew, with the exception of the chief officer, who was probably killed in the attack, to get away in the boats. Later in the morning they were picked up by the destroyer *Viscount* and landed at Liverpool on the 5th.

The Vice Commodore's ship *Victoria City*, which had dropped out of the convoy on 26 November due to the bad weather, was never seen again and it is believed she was sunk by Hans-Peter Hinsch in *U-140*. Wreckage identified with her was washed up on the Irish coast on 8 December, but of her forty-three crew members there was no trace.

HX 90's escort force finally arrived as the sun was rising on the morning of the 2nd. The ragged remains of the convoy re-formed and continued on its way eastwards. But the agony was not yet over for the remaining merchant ships, now labouring in a south-westerly gale. A far-ranging Focke-Wulf Condor sighted the convoy, and at 1000 came in to the attack, bombing and sinking the 4360-ton *W. Hendrick*, and wounding two men on board the *Quebec City* with machine-gun fire. That afternoon Otto Kretschmer and Herbert Kuppisch returned, and despite the efforts of the hard-pressed escorts, sank the 6022-ton *Stirlingshire* and the Norwegian ship *Samanger* of 4276 tons. Later, after dark, Kuppisch came back for what would be the final assault on the convoy, sinking the 6725-ton Glasgow ship *Wilhelmina*.

When it was all over, the reckoning could be done. Convoy HX 90 had been under almost continuous attack for twenty-six hours, most of this time completely unprotected by the Royal Navy. A total of eleven ships of nearly 60,000 tons had been lost and three other ships damaged. For the U-boats, who apparently suffered no casualties, it was a cheap victory, and a victory of the first magnitude. For the merchant seamen who survived it had been a fearful nightmare they would have to live with for the rest of their lives. For the dead, there was nothing but a cold, unmarked grave.

The war was kinder to Ernst Mengersen. In *U-101*, and later in *U-607*, he sank a further 58,361 tons of Allied shipping, and eventually received the Knight's Cross and promotion to

Korvettenkapitän. He survived to see the surrender of the U-boats in 1945 and lived on into retirement.

Günther Prien, whose intervention in the *Dunsley*'s rescue bid led to the deaths of the men of the *Lady Glanely*, was not so fortunate. After a five-hour duel with the destroyer HMS *Wolverine* off Rockall on 7 March 1941 *U-47* was caught by a salvo of ten depth charges and blew up under water. Prien and all his men perished. For the *Lady Glanely* justice had been done.

10

Against Two Enemies

January 1941 was the month of the Focke-Wulf Condor in the Battle of the Atlantic. Since the previous summer the Germans had been using these giant four-engined aircraft, which had a range of over 2000 miles, as scouts for the U-boat Arm, spotting and shadowing convoys from a safe distance while homing in the U-boats by radio. With Britain unable to provide air cover for her ships in the Atlantic, the Condors, bristling with guns and carrying a bomb-load of 4,500 lbs, then assumed a more aggressive role, searching out and attacking convoy stragglers and ships sailing independently. In the first month of 1941 they sank twenty Allied ships totalling 78,517 tons.

Halifax, the capital of Nova Scotia, sits on a peninsula overlooking two magnificent deep-water bays. The outer bay, sheltered from the rigours of the Atlantic, is 10 miles square and free from ice all year round, making it, in 1941, the ideal North American assembly point for convoys bound for Britain. In this quiet haven, on 12 January of that year, twenty-five merchant ships lay at anchor awaiting the signal to begin their battle with the dangers, natural and man-made, which stalked the open water beyond the headlands. This was Convoy SC 19, scheduled to cross the North Atlantic at 7½-8 knots, weather permitting – and in January it rarely did.

Escorts were still in short supply and SC 19 would have in support only the armed merchant cruiser *Aurania*, an ex-passenger ship of 13,984 tons. The odds against the convoy surviving the Atlantic passage unharmed were short, for the enemy's naval activity in these waters was at a peak. The 11-inch gun pocket battleship *Admiral Scheer*, which had caused havoc in Convoy HX 84 two months earlier, and the 18,200-ton cruiser *Admiral Hipper* were both at large and, augmenting the usual complement of U-boats, were eight Italian long-range submarines. To this was added the increasing threat of the Focke-Wulf Condors.

For Captain C.F. Linton, master of Goulds Steamships' *Grelrosa*, pocket battleships and U-boats were mere incidental dangers. His 27-year-old, 4574-ton ship was loaded down to her marks with a full cargo of wheat and he considered that the North Atlantic would constitute the greatest threat once he put to sea. From early that morning he had watched the barometer falling steeply and felt the wind freshening from the east, indicating to him that a depression was on its way up from Cape Hatteras. By late afternoon, with the convoy preparing to sail, it was blowing a full gale, even in the shelter of the bay. Outside the headlands the hounds of Hell were being let loose.

With night coming on, Linton's seaman's instinct urged him to postpone the sailing until next morning, and he would have done so had the choice been his. The Canadian pilot who boarded to take the *Grelrosa* out of harbour was of a similar opinion and, after conferring with Linton, returned ashore to put their joint views to the Naval Control. Characteristically, the Navy brushed aside the opinions of two merchant seamen, which were based on a thorough understanding of the awesome power of the sea and the limitations of the average merchant ship. Regardless of the weather, the convoy would sail that afternoon. It was a decision the Navy would regret.

SC 19 sailed from Halifax at 1600 and, not unexpectedly, once clear of the harbour ran into the full force of a howling easterly gale that all but blew the struggling ships back into the bay. The light was already failing and the visibility reduced by driving snow. An attempt was made to form up the convoy in its predetermined nine columns abreast, but this proved to be a pointless exercise. When darkness fell, SC 19 was still a confused jumble of ships, battered by heavy seas, in visibility of less than half a mile, and more occupied with avoiding collision with each other than with the irrelevant business of assuming a tidy formation.

During the night the gale backed to the north-west, but with no abatement. By the morning of the 13th the visibility had improved somewhat, but the snow squalls were as fierce as ever. The convoy had resolved into three widely scattered groups of ships, the *Grelrosa* finding herself in company with five others. In between squalls Linton caught sight of the leading ships of the convoy and decided to make a determined effort to catch up with them. The ageing *Grelrosa*'s best speed in fine weather was 8 knots, but in the conditions prevailing the task Linton set her was beyond her capability. By the afternoon of the 14th she had not only failed to join the leaders but, with the snow showers merging to become a white curtain reducing visibility near to zero, she had lost all contact with the other ships. She was alone on an extremely hostile sea.

At the Commodore's conference prior to sailing Linton was provided with the convoy route and various rendezvous positions to make for should he become separated from the convoy. He now had no other option than to proceed independently, making for each rendezvous point in turn with the hope of eventually rejoining the main body of the ships. There was no let-up in the weather and as the *Grelrosa* edged doggedly to the north-east the temperature fell steadily. Soon ice was forming on the decks and around the accommodation, adding discomfort to the never-ending punishment of the pounding waves and heaving swell. Sextants were kept handy on the bridge, but it seemed that the sun and stars had disappeared for ever and all navigation was reduced to dead reckoning.

During the first three days Linton took comfort from occasional wireless message heard from the *Aurania*, but the transmissions began to fade and he assumed the *Grelrosa* must be gradually falling further astern. But he had underestimated the capabilities of his ship. Convoy SC 19, having gathered together nineteen ships, was only making good an average speed of 5½ knots, compared with the *Grelrosa*'s steady 6 knots. In poor visibility, Linton's ship had actually overtaken the convoy and was drawing ahead at the rate of half a mile every hour.

For another eight days the foul weather continued and the *Grelrosa* plodded on alone. Then, on the 25th, a slow improvement set in. By the 28th, when she was around 200 miles from the west coast of Ireland, the wind and sea dropped away and the sun shone fitfully out of a cloudy sky. His ship having endured and survived the worst efforts of the North Atlantic, Linton was able to turn his mind to the other dangers which would inevitably threaten during the forty-eight hours to come. The *Grelrosa* was now in the north-western approaches to the British Isles, in waters infested with predatory U-boats and within easy reach of German long-range bombers based in Western France. She was slow and ungainly, and was unlikely to be able to run away from trouble when it came. To defend herself she had a 4-inch anti-submarine gun and a 12-pounder aft, with two Hotchkiss .303 machine guns on the bridge. The heavier guns were manned by DEMS gunners, who could be relied on to give a good account of themselves if the opportunity arose. For the time being it only remained to keep a sharp lookout for danger.

The attack came from the air on the morning of the 28th. At 1000 the *Grelrosa*'s second officer, who had the watch on the bridge, sighted an aircraft flying low over the water on the port bow. Unable to identify the plane as friend or foe, he prudently sounded the signal for aircraft attack on the steam whistle. When Captain Linton reached the bridge the aircraft was circling at some distance from the ship. It was a four-engined, black-painted machine, which looked ominous and alien to Linton. He ordered the guns to be manned, instructing the gunners to hold their fire until the plane made an obvious move towards the ship. Hardly had his orders been complied with than the aircraft – now identified as a Focke-Wulf Condor – came roaring in at mast-top height, its bomb doors open.

The *Grelrosa*'s 12-pounder opened up with a sharp crack, but ceased fire after two rounds, as the Focke-Wulf was already below the maximum depression of the gun. Unharmed, the big black aircraft swept in from the port quarter, spraying the bridge with its forward turret and releasing a bomb as it crossed the after deck from port to starboard. There was a heavy explosion and Linton, taking cover behind the bulwark of the bridge wing, watched as the *Grelrosa*'s mainmast toppled and fell, taking with it the ship's wireless aerials. The Focke-Wulf then circled briefly before making a second attack, this time approaching from right astern. Three more bombs rained down, the first crashing through the engine-room skylight and completely wrecking the engine spaces. The second hit the cross-bunker hatch, burying itself in the coal before exploding, while the third fell harmlessly into the sea on the port side of the bridge.

As the aircraft roared over the length of the ship its forward and after gun turrets raked the the decks and superstructure. The fire was returned by the bridge Hotchkiss guns, enthusiastically manned by the Second and Third Officers, while this time the 12-pounder managed to get off five rounds, one of which was seen to burst directly in front of the plane. Linton saw his Third Officer die, cut down by his own ammunition when the enemy's bullets exploded amongst it. Perhaps damaged, or just satisfied with the carnage it had wrought, the Focke-Wulf then flew off towards the horizon.

The *Grelrosa* was listing heavily to starboard and settling in the water, and it required only a brief examination to convince Linton that she was finished, her engine smashed, her hull blasted open to the sea. His Third Officer was dead, his Chief and Third Engineers badly wounded, and two men missing.

Linton did what he could to make the injured men comfortable and ordered the rest of his crew to prepare to abandon ship. This was not to be the simple operation practised at weekly boat drills. The bomb which had wrecked the *Grelrosa*'s engine-room had also torn her two lifeboats from their davits and hurled them into the sea, where they now floated alongside, half-submerged. Fortunately the ship carried two small jolly boats – little more than dinghies – one on each side of the bridge. Linton ordered these to be lowered and provisioned from the smashed lifeboats. The one remaining serviceable liferaft was also put over the side. While all this was being done, Radio Officer P.T. O'Keith rigged a jury aerial and, using the portable lifeboat transmitter, attempted to get away a distress message.

When the boats were ready Linton ordered O'Keith to leave with the rest of the crew, but the radio officer refused to go until

73

he was sure his SOS had been heard. The *Grelrosa*'s chief steward, A. Burn, who was doing his best to comfort the injured engineers, neither of whom could be moved, also refused to go to the boats. Linton, who had already decided he would not leave the injured men while the ship still floated, pleaded with O'Keith and Burn to save themselves, but the two men shook their heads and carried on with their work. With the ship now listing dangerously, Linton feared she would soon capsize, but eventually the situation solved itself. O'Keith heard an acknowledgement to his SOS and the gravely injured Chief Engineer died. Linton and the others then put the Third Engineer onto a damaged raft, hoping he would float off when the ship sank, and finally went over the side at 1130. The *Grelrosa* went down half an hour later.

Linton split up his remaining men between the two small boats and the one undamaged liferaft. The jolly boats were leaking and badly overcrowded, but fortunately the sea was quiet. The Third Engineer was taken from his raft when it floated clear and made as comfortable as possible in the bottom of one of the boats, but he died soon afterwards. There being no room for Linton and Burn in the jolly boats or on a raft, they took refuge in one of the waterlogged lifeboats.

The bravery and persistence of Radio Officer O'Keith, who had refused to leave the ship until he had alerted the outside world to their fate, was rewarded next morning with the arrival of the destroyer HMS *Volunteer*. All thirty-one survivors were picked up and landed safely at Greenock.

The rest of Convoy SC 19 did not escape unscathed. The Focke-Wulf responsible for sinking the *Grelrosa* on the 28th informed Lorient of the position of the main body of the convoy and at about 0300 on the 29th the U-boats moved in. In quick succession *U-93*, commanded by Kapitänleutnant Claus Korth, torpedoed and sank three ships, including the 10,468-ton British tanker *W.B. Walker*, before being chased off by the destroyers which had arrived to escort SC 19 into the North Channel.

Around this time the 4354-ton *West Wales* was wallowing along 12 miles astern of the convoy. Like the *Grelrosa* she had had no contact with SC 19 since shortly after leaving Halifax. At about 0550 on the 29th she was sighted by Herbert Kuppisch in *U-94*, who had been frustrated in his efforts to attack SC 19. One torpedo into the starboard side of the *West Wales* was sufficient to stop her dead in her tracks, sinking by the bow. Captain Frederick Nicholls ordered his men into the boats at once. As the boats were being lowered, Kuppisch fired a second torpedo from a range of no more than 100 yards and the crippled ship sank almost immediately, leaving many of her crew struggling in the water.

When a destroyer arrived on the scene about ten minutes later, it was able to picked up seventeen men from the lifeboats. A second destroyer subsequently rescued Captain Nicholls and four others from the sea, but Nicholls died soon after being picked up. Of the *West Wales'* crew of thirty-seven, in all sixteen men died on that cold January morning 120 miles to the southwest of the lonely Atlantic island they call Rockall.

U-94 escaped the attentions of the British destroyers and went on to create more havoc amongst Allied shipping. She was eventually sunk in a combined operation by the Canadian destroyer *Oakville* and aircraft of the US Squadron 92 off the West Indies in August 1942. Herbert Kuppisch was not in command at the time. His final reckoning came a year later, when, on 27 August 1943, he was lost with the auxilliary tanker *U-847* when she was sunk by aircraft from the US carrier *Card* some 300 miles to the west of the Azores.

11

The Straggler

In the early months of 1941 the noose thrown around the British sea lanes by the U-boats was tightening relentlessly. The total of Allied shipping lost had reached 4,750,000 tons, and the upward trend seemed unstoppable. Ships were now being sunk faster than replacements could be built and, for a nation whose survival in the war required the annual importation of 43 million tons of cargo, time was surely running out.

The first day of February opened with the sinking in the North Atlantic of the 4351-ton Greek ship *Nicolaos Angelos*, announcing the return to sea of Kapitänleutnant Herbert Schultze and *U-48* after an absence of almost twelve months. Schultze was now one of Germany's most successful U-boat commanders and the despatch of the *Nicolaos Angelos* brought his score to almost 95,000 tons. One more decent-sized ship sent to the bottom would see him past the magical 100,000-ton mark and would certainly lead to the award of the long overdue Knight's Cross on his return to Germany. This tantalizing prospect must have been high in Schultze's mind as he cruised south-south-east towards the Western Approaches.

Two days before the sinking of the *Nicolaos Angelos*, and 3000 miles to the south, Convoy SLS 64 was assembling at an anchorage in the shadow of the densely forested hills of Sierra Leone. SLS 64 was a slow convoy, with a planned speed of only 7½ knots and an estimated passage time of nineteen days from Freetown to Oban, where its ships would join coastal convoys for their various ports of discharge. And as if the disadvantage of its slow speed was not handicap enough, SLS 64 was to be accorded the doubtful privilege of being completely unescorted. For the twenty ageing tramps involved, the convoy would be little more than a gesture of solidarity between them. It seemed that the Admiralty, in its wisdom, preferred the ships to take their chance in company, rather than alone.

Among those about to commit herself to the make-believe security of Convoy SLS 64 was the 24-year-old *Nailsea Lass*, a steamer of 4289 tons. She was a typical British tramp of her day, Bristol Channel based, and showing the effects of many long years service in the cross-trades. She had left the United Kingdom in April of the previous year and was now, nine months later, on her way home with 6,200 tons of produce from India. It had been a long and arduous voyage, and no one was more pleased to be about to embark on the final leg than the *Nailsea Lass*' master, Captain Thomas Bradford. But while he was not averse to accepting the hospitality of the convoy, he had serious doubts about his ship's ability to stand the pace, even at 7½ knots. She had seen her best years and was a long time out of dry dock, her bottom being badly fouled by weed and shell which had their origins in the warm waters of the East. At the very best, Bradford estimated, his ship would do well to maintain a bare 7 knots on the passage north; with a head wind, which was to be expected at this time of the year, somewhat less. The possibility of sailing independently must have occurred to Captain Bradford but, as it turned out, the choice was to be made for him.

While the *Nailsea Lass* sweltered in the lee of Cape Sierra Leone, the 8-inch gun cruiser *Admiral Hipper* was at her berth in the Biscay port of Brest preparing to set out on her second sortie of the war. Her first adventure had almost ended in disaster when, on Christmas Day 1940, she was badly mauled while attacking a heavily escorted troop convoy off the Azores. Subsequent to this débâcle, the German cruiser, which had a notoriously low cruising range for her size, was limited to short patrols in the vicinity of her refuelling tanker, based some 1000 miles west of the Bay of Biscay. When she left Brest in early January, it was with orders to attack only lightly escorted convoys or merchant ships sailing alone.

SLS 64 left Freetown on the morning of 30 January, an

organized assembly of ships, but without the real means to defend itself against a determined foe. Most of the ships were armed, but only with the usual assortment of obsolete relics left over from the First World War. The *Nailsea Lass* was no exception. Her quiver of arrows contained an ancient 4-inch, two Lewis guns and a strange device known as a Holman Projector. This was the product of the fevered imagination of a well-intentioned but somewhat naive boffin, a crude form of mortar connected to the ship's deck steam line and designed to fire hand grenades at low-flying aircraft. The average merchant ship's deck steam being a most unpredictable form of propulsion, most grenades fired, after climbing 20 or 30 feet into the air, fell back to explode on deck, much to the consternation of the operator.

The Holman Projector's only real claim to utility lay in providing amusement for bored ships' gunners, who used it to fire rotten potatoes at adjacent ships in the convoy.

Captain Bradford's fears about his ship's ability to maintain convoy speed were soon realized. In spite of the determined efforts of the *Nailsea Lass*' engineers, her foul bottom held her back from the start and by nightfall on the first day at sea she was straggling astern of the convoy. When dawn broke on 1 February the other ships were out of sight over the horizon. Philosophically, Thomas Bradford accepted that he was now reduced to sailing home alone and consoled himself with the thought that the *Nailsea Lass* was probably as safe on her own as in the company of an unescorted convoy, if not safer. He was proved right. Thirteen days out of Freetown, when passing 150 miles east of the Azores, SLS 64 was pounced upon by the waiting *Admiral Hipper*. In a very short space of time the heavy cruiser sank seven ships totalling 32,806 tons. She might well have taken the rest of the fleeing convoy, but she was running short of fuel and was forced to break off the attack and return to Brest.

Unaware of her providential escape, the *Nailsea Lass* pushed steadily north at her best speed of 6 knots. On the 16th, when abeam of the Straits of Gibraltar, she made her first contact with the rest of the world, when a patrolling British warship intercepted her, but made off at speed after a brief exchange of signals. A few hours later the *Nailsea Lass* ran into a strong head gale, and was soon burying her blunt bows in an angry sea, her speed reduced to 3 knots. To her crew it seemed like the all too familiar welcome home to northern waters. Eight days later, on the evening of the 24th, the *Nailsea Lass* was 60 miles to the south-west of the Fastnet Rock and heading up towards the North Channel, wartime gateway to the British ports. The weather had turned fine, with good visibility and only a light wind and low swell to disturb the surface of the sea. The first stirrings of approaching spring were in the air, but the night was cold.

At fifteen minutes before eight o'clock Chief Officer Alfred Hodder paced the wing of the bridge feeling more than content with his lot. The last minutes of the watch were ticking away, one of the few remaining watches he would have to stand in this passage, which had already lasted twenty-six days. The threat of the enemy, too, was receding, for very soon the *Nailsea Lass* would come under the protection of the warships and aircraft guarding the Western Approaches. In a few days, if no unforeseen disaster occurred, she would be safe in port, and all the tensions and fears of the long, lonely voyage would disperse as the fog does with the touch of a warm sun.

Hodder's dream of that other world was rudely shattered when the *Nailsea Lass* staggered under a sledgehammer blow, closely followed by a bang like a clap of thunder. Momentarily deafened, Hodder watched a huge column of water erupt from the port side of the ship abreast the forward masthouse. As the column toppled and the sea began to rain down on the bridge, he dived for the engine-room telegraph and swung the handle to the stop position. The wounded ship vibrated roughly as her engine slowed abruptly and ground to a halt. She took an ominous list to port as the water poured into her holds.

When the torpedo struck, Second Officer Ernest Knight was in his cabin below the bridge preparing to turn in. As is the lot of second officers in merchant ships, he had the punishing middle watch, midnight to 4 am, which condemned him to a night of broken sleep on every night the ship was at sea. When the *Nailsea Lass* heeled over to starboard and the explosion came,

Knight was at once aware that on this night there would be no need for him to go through the usual routine of courting sleep while the rest of the ship was awake. As he reached for his life-jacket, he heard from the bridge Captain Bradford giving the order to abandon ship. Knight's next movements were almost automatic. Sprinting up the bridge ladder, he hurried into the dimly lit chartroom and began to bundle up the ship's secret code and signal books into the weighted bag kept handy. As he was so engaged, he felt the ship tipping by the bow and lost no time in tumbling out onto the deck. He ran to the rail and hurled the Admiralty's secrets into the sea below. His primary duty done, he gave thought to his own survival.

Reaching the boat deck, Knight was surprised to learn that there had been no casualties, despite the fact that, in the style of her day, the *Nailsea Lass* housed her ratings under the forecastle head, not many feet forward of where she had been hit. With the weather still in a kindly mood, the ship was abandoned in an orderly fashion, all thirty-six men getting away in the two lifeboats. It was just as well they had wasted no time in taking to the boats, for as they pulled clear the stern of the ship reared up and she went down bow-first. The chartroom clock showed exactly 2000 as the water closed over it, but there would be no change of the watch in the *Nailsea Lass* that night – or ever again.

As the men lay back on their oars, mourning the loss of their ship, Kapitänleutnant Herbert Schultze took one last precaution-ary look through his periscope and gave the order to blow tanks. Second Officer Ernest Knight, at the tiller of the Captain's boat, sucked in his breath as *U-48*, her black hull cascading water, surfaced close by, then motored over to Chief Officer Hodder's boat. The U-boat commander appeared in the conning tower and Knight heard him, speaking in good English, order Hodder to bring his boat alongside. Hodder obeyed and, after a short exchange with Schultze, boarded the submarine and disappeared below. Being aware of the German Navy's policy of pulling senior merchant ships' officers out of circulation, Knight knew he was unlikely to see Hodder again until after the war.

It was Captain Bradford's turn next for, with a flurry of white water at her stern, the U-boat was approaching. Rising and falling on the swell, the boat bumped heavily on the submarine casing as she came alongside. As Knight ordered his crew to fend off, his eyes met Bradford's and an unspoken farewell passed between them.

The lifeboat drifted astern until it was abreast the U-boat's conning tower and Knight looked up to see Herbert Schultze, a tall figure in a white-topped cap, leaning over the rail. Schultze first inquired if there were any injured in the boat, then, in conversation with Bradford – who had made no attempt to conceal his rank – expressed his regret at having to sink the *Nailsea Lass*. Nevertheless, he took Bradford prisoner and motored away into the night.

With Captain Bradford and Chief Officer Hodder having been whisked away into captivity, Ernest Knight now found himself in command of the survivors of the *Nailsea Lass*. He immediately closed the other lifeboat, now in the charge of 19-year-old Third Officer Gouge, to discuss their plight. He discovered that Schultze had given Gouge two packets of cigarettes and a course for the nearest land – a poor exchange for the loss of a ship and her two senior men. While the cigarettes were appreciated, the course was of little use to Gouge, as his compass had been damaged by the blast of the torpedo.

Knight now had to decide whether to lash the two boats together and remain in the vicinity of the sinking, awaiting rescue, or to set a course for the land. The prospect of an early search being made for them was extremely unlikely, as the *Nailsea Lass*' wireless transmitter had been smashed and no SOS was sent out before she sank. Not surprisingly, Knight opted to make for the Irish coast, a little over 60 miles to the north-east. There was insufficient wind to fill the sails, so the two boats set off rowing in close company.

At midnight the wind freshened from the south-west and, with the hope of an early landing increasing, sail was hoisted and the boats ran free before the wind. During the course of the night they became separated and Knight decided to press on alone. By late afternoon on the 25th he had the land in sight. But darkness was then closing in and, as the wind and sea were rising, it seemed prudent to heave-to and wait for daylight before approaching the coast.

Further south, Gouge had arrived at the same decision, but tragedy was now stalking the men of the *Nailsea Lass*. A depression moving in quickly from the Atlantic brought a fierce gale which, accompanied by driving rain, added to the discomfort of the bitterly cold night. Before morning came five men, three firemen, an ordinary seaman and the cook, had died of exposure in the half-swamped lifeboats. For them it was a cold and miserable death, a cruel ending to a long voyage that had climaxed in the loss of their ship, their belongings and their dignity.

Although the *Nailsea Lass* was long gone under, with five of her men now dead and two in captivity, her survivors continued the fight to live and sail again. Knight succeeded in bringing his boat through the Blasket Sound to land at Ballyoughtraugh in County Kerry on the morning of the 26th. A few hours later 19-year-old Gouge, who had seen four men die in his boat during the night, gained the shelter of Bantry Bay and made the shore at Bere Haven. It was a day short of a month since they sailed from Freetown in the company of Convoy SL 64.

A jubilant Herbert Schultze brought *U-48* into Brest eleven days later, where he was duly presented with the Knight's Cross by Admiral Dönitz. By the end of March *U-48* and Schultze had returned to sea to sink another 49,363 tons of Allied shipping, before the submarine was taken out of service in the summer of that year. Herbert Schultze survived the war, attaining the rank of Kapitän-zur-See. *U-48* came to an ignominious end, being scuttled in a North German port ahead of the Allied advance in May 1945.

12

Death in the
St George's Channel

Following the capitulation of France in June 1940, Germany gained control of an additional 800 miles of Atlantic coastline, stretching from the Dover Strait to Northern Spain. This was a catastrophic blow for the hard-pressed ships of the Royal Navy. The scratching of the pens on the surrender document in that historic railway carriage in the forest of Compiègne in effect moved the U-boats a thousand miles nearer to their hunting grounds off the west coast of Ireland. Relocated in the Biscay ports of Brest, Lorient, St Nazaire and Bordeaux, they had access to the whole of the Atlantic, with a reduced risk of attack on passage and an immense saving in time and fuel on their voyaging to and from the convoy lanes.

The Admiralty quickly offset some of this advantage by laying an extensive minefield in the Western Approaches, effectively sealing off both the St George's Channel and the English Channel from the south and west. All shipping bound for British ports was then routed further north, in through the North Channel between Scotland and Northern Ireland, or around the north of Scotland if bound for East Coast ports. The time during which the Atlantic convoys were vulnerable to attack by U-boats was thus considerably shortened.

One ship to gain particular benefit from this isolation of the St George's Channel behind the minefield was the 1922-ton cross-channel steamer *St Patrick*, which had hitherto been making the 54-mile passage between Fishguard and Rosslare under constant threat of U-boat attack. Owned by the Fishguard & Rosslare Railways and Harbours Company, and commanded by Captain James Faraday, the *St Patrick* kept open a tenuous but vital link between Britain and neutral Eire, carrying passengers and cargo.

Although the St George's Channel was made safe from the attentions of the U-boats, it was still open to the long-range Focke-Wulf Condors and Ju88s of the Luftwaffe based at Stavanger and Bordeaux. The *St Patrick* was bombed and machine-gunned by one of these aircraft in August 1940, but escaped without serious damage or casualties. Now, whenever she attempted the short crossing between Fishguard and Rosslare, which was on a daily basis, she went to sea on full alert.

Seafaring is a hazardous calling at the best of times and it is not surprising that those who follow it are superstitious by nature. They have always been of the opinion that leaving port on a Friday, with all its associations with the Crucifixion, is not a sensible thing to do. Should that Friday happen to be the thirteenth day of the month, their willingness to venture out to sea is doubly grudging. Even in this present age of hard-nosed reality, shipmasters are still known to find excuses for not sailing on Friday the Thirteenth.

As master of a cross-channel steamer committed to a tight schedule, Captain James Faraday was unable to allow himself the luxury of indulging in such unprofessional manipulation. Shortly before one o'clock on the morning of Friday 13 June 1941 the *St Patrick*, having embarked her passengers and cargo, left her berth in Rosslare harbour as scheduled. Weather permitting, and the report was favourable, Faraday was confident of arriving in Fishguard in ample time to connect with the London boat train at 0600.

When she cleared the breakwaters of Rosslare the *St Patrick* met with fine, clear weather, with only a light wind blowing – a perfect early summer's night. Captain Faraday looked forward to a quiet crossing, his opinion being that the minefield to the south and the Navy's anti-submarine patrols had made this stretch of water as safe as it could be. There was, of course, the danger of attack by enemy aircraft, as his ship had found out some ten months earlier, but the possibility of lightning striking twice in the same place seemed remote. The *St Patrick* was fast and the crossing short. The ship would be vulnerable only for three hours or so, between dawn and the time she found shelter behind the breakwaters of Fishguard harbour. Hopefully, the formalities there would be as brief as usual, and Faraday was already anticipating the brisk walk to the village, where his wife would have breakfast ready in the big house overlooking the harbour. He would be accompanied on that walk by his young son Jack, a Merchant Navy cadet on leave from his own ship and passenger in the *St Patrick*. Of Faraday's three sons, all of whom were serving their country, Jack was the only one to adopt his father's chosen profession and therefore held a special place in the Captain's affections.

At 0426 on the morning of the 13th the *St Patrick* was 10 miles off Strumble Head, the steep headland that marks the southern extremity of Cardigan Bay, and slicing her way through the water towards Fishguard, 14 miles to the south-east. The sun was just twenty minutes below the horizon, its first rays already fingering the clear sky. The usual early morning onshore breeze had arisen, kicking up whitecaps on the still-dark surface of the sea, but they did nothing to impede the ferry on the last few miles of her passage. Pacing the bridge, James Faraday was savouring the satisfaction of another voyage completed on time and without incident. Below, in the passenger accommodation, a few restless travellers stirred, but the majority slept on while the two stewardesses, Jane Hughes and May Owen, prepared for the coming disembarkation.

There was no prior warning of the attack. The German aircraft came in from the dark side, unseen by the bridge look-outs or the men manning the 12-pounder gun on the dawn stand-to. Either by good luck or uncanny good judgement, the stick of four bombs landed squarely on the cross-bunker fuel tanks, which ran the breadth of the ship immediately forward of her funnel. The *St Patrick* erupted in a ball of fire and began to sink at once.

The massive explosion wiped out the first-class accommodation on the boat deck, killing all its occupants except one.

Stewardess Jane Hughes died with them. Ironically, the less privileged passengers below decks fared better, although they suffered a frightening ordeal. They found themselves in complete darkness, with the ship listing heavily, and overall was the cloying stench of fuel oil escaping from the ruptured bunker tanks. As the living tried to grope their way through the maze of unfamiliar alleyways and ladders, the crackle of flames added to their fears. A group of frightened women in the lowest deck seemed doomed to go down with the ship until Stewardess May Owen, with complete disregard for her own life, fought her way through the chaos and led them to safety on deck.

It was very fortunate that, on this occasion, the *St Patrick*'s crew outnumbered her passengers by forty-five to forty-four, for within seven minutes of being hit the ship was her way to the bottom. Captain Faraday's men, and one remaining woman, acted with magnificent courage and cool efficiency. It was possible to launch only one of the ship's lifeboats, this being quickly dropped to the water manned by two seamen. Those passengers who had survived the bombing had to be coaxed into the water, some requiring considerable persuasion, for the wind had risen and the sea was developing an angry chop. The boat, with Steward George Walters at the tiller, plucked thirty survivors from the water, while other seamen swam around dragging the terrified passengers on to liferafts. Many of those rescued were covered with black oil, which was escaping from the *St Patrick*'s tanks and adding further agony to this tragedy at sunrise.

Stewardess May Owen refused to leave the ship until she had seen all her women passengers into their lifejackets and over the side. She was about to leave herself when she heard the cries of another woman still below decks. Although she realized the ship had only a few minutes to live, May Owen went below again, brought the woman up on deck and jumped over the side with her. Neither woman had a lifejacket and for the next two hours the stewardess supported the passenger in the rough, oil-covered sea until both were pulled onto a raft.

Second Engineer Frank Purcell, who had already saved three of his men trapped in the engine-room after the bombing, also rescued a wounded fellow crew member and kept him afloat until they reached a liferaft. Young Jack Faraday, a strong swimmer, had no difficulty in getting way from the sinking ship. It would have been easy for him to join the others on the rafts, but when he discovered that his father was missing he swam back towards the blazing wreck. Neither Jack nor his father were seen again.

At 0433 on the morning of Friday 13 June, as the rays of the rising sun were striking fire from the hills to the east of Fishguard Bay, the *St Patrick* slipped below the waves with a fierce hissing of quenched fires. Sixty-five men, women and children were left to fight for their lives against an increasingly angry sea.

Ashore, in the busy Fishguard harbour complex where the boat train from London came down to the sea, there was a noticeable air of unease. The *St Patrick* was overdue and many an anxious eye was turned towards her empty berth. It would appear that, although the attack on the ferry took place only 10 miles off Strumble Head, nothing had been seen, or reported, by the lighthouse keepers. Concern for the *St Patrick*'s safety was increased when, in a flurry of spray, the Fishguard lifeboat, *Whitestar*, roared down the slipway and headed out through the breakwaters at full speed. Word went around that an un-identified ship was on fire off Strumble Head.

Circling to the north-west of Strumble, the lifeboat found an ominous-looking patch of oil on the water, a few pieces wreckage that could have been just flotsam, but no lifeboats, no rafts, no survivors. Stopping only to pick up two fish boxes seen floating in the vicinity of the oil slick, *Whitestar* headed back for Fishguard, concluding that some unfortunate fishing boat had foundered, taking all hands with her. It was only when the lifeboat was back in harbour that the fears of those on shore began to move towards awful reality. The fish boxes were identi-fied by their markings as being from the *St Patrick*'s cargo. The *Whitestar* returned to sea at once to resume the search, but it was now apparent to all involved that some terrible calamity had overcome the Fishguard to Rosslare ferry.

If there is a special god who watches over seamen, then he must surely have been in the vicinity of Strumble Head on that

June morning in 1941. When the *St Patrick* sank, seven minutes after being hit by the stick of bombs, she left behind her sixty-five survivors. Thirty were crammed into a lifeboat, while the rest were on, or clinging to, liferafts, which were being constantly capsized by the rough seas. Many of the survivors were covered in black fuel oil, all were cold, wretched and frightened. Those who knew, took comfort from the fact that the *St Patrick*'s wireless operator had been able to get away an SOS before she sank. Also, the ship had been on fire in sight of Strumble Head lighthouse when she went down. Rescue, probably in the form of the Fishguard lifeboat, stationed only 14 miles away, must surely already be on the way. An hour passed, then two, but there was no sign of the familiar blue and white craft speeding towards them.

It seems likely that, had these wretched people been condemned to await the arrival of the lifeboat, many of them would have died, for Fishguard was not then aware of their predicament. As luck – or that special seaman's god – would have it, a convoy was passing off the coast at the time of the sinking and the *St Patrick*'s SOS was answered by the convoy's escorts. Just over two hours after they had been cast into the sea, the sixty-five survivors were picked up. Three hours later they were landed at Milford Haven and word was flashed to Fishguard harbour. For the people of Fishguard and the surrounding villages, where most of the ferry's crew lived, the news of the rescue brought blessed relief, but there could be little rejoicing. It was though a dark cloud had drifted in over Fishguard Bay. Never again would the little *St Patrick* be seen trailing her plume of smoke through the breakwaters. Captain James Faraday would walk the harbour road no more, neither would his gallant son Jack. Jane Hughes was dead and so were fifteen men of the area. Friday 13 June 1941, a day which brought grief to many, widowhood to some, and made orphans of the innocent, would be remembered with horror for many years to come.

On a grey afternoon in November 1982 the Sealink ferry *Stena Normandica*, then employed on the Fishguard to Rosslare service, lay hove to 10 miles off Strumble Head in clear sight of its white-painted lighthouse, as had the burning *St Patrick* forty-one years earlier. With only the melancholy cries of the wheeling gulls as an accompaniment, a brief service was held and a wreath of flowers cast on the water in remembrance of those who lost their lives in the wartime ferry. It was a sad reflection on the state of Britain's merchant fleet that the flag at the dip at the *Stena Normandica*'s stern was not the Red Ensign but the blue and yellow of Sweden. How the ghosts of those who died for their country within sight of its rocky shores must have wept on that day – not for their lost years, but for a maritime heritage that was no more.

13

America Lends a Hand

The bombing of Pearl Harbor by the Japanese in December 1941 finally brought a hitherto reluctant United States of America into the war. Within a few days of Pearl Harbor Admiral Dönitz, always alert to new opportunities, moved a small force of his U-boats into the far-Western Atlantic. The US Navy, lacking experience in anti-submarine warfare, found itself easily outwitted by these savage marauders. Operating close in to the American seaboard, from New York to the Caribbean, the Germans sank over 100 ships of 750,000 tons in the first four months of 1942. Only one U-boat was lost.

The campaign gave birth to a new crop of U-boat aces, among them Korvettenkapitän Johann Mohr, who commanded *U-124*. Unfortunately for Mohr and his fellow submariners, the Americans characteristically brought their defences into order at once and the U-boats were forced to retire to the mid-Atlantic. By the end of April, Mohr with nine sinkings to his credit, was to be found haunting the northern convoy route in the vicinity of 29 degrees West. He was accompanied by Kapitänleutnant Hans-Peter Hinsch in *U-569* and Kapitänleutnant Otto Ites in *U-94*.

Eight hundred miles to the east of the German trio's search area lay the island of Islay, in the Inner Hebrides. Islay boasts one of the only Celtic churches in Scotland, a host of whisky distilleries and a climate ranging from the miserable to the malignant, for there is nothing but 2000 miles of uninterrupted Atlantic Ocean to the west of the island. Loch Indaal, a deep, bay-like fjord which all but cuts Islay in two, provides the only shelter from the ocean.

On the morning of 7 May 1942 the tiny whitewashed cottages overlooking Loch Indaal witnessed the assembling of Convoy ONS 92. By noon that day a total of forty-one merchant ships, most of them riding light, had gathered in the grey waters of the loch. Two hours later the merchantmen were joined by their escorts for the coming voyage, a combined force of US and Canadian naval ships, which had earlier set out from Lough Foyle, on the other side of the North Channel. Flags raced up halyards, signal lamps clattered and, within the hour, ONS 92 was steaming westwards to the granaries and arsenals of North America.

Occupying an uncomfortably exposed position in the middle of the port outer column of ONS 92 was the steamer *Llanover*, owned by Evan Thomas, Radcliffe & Company and commanded by Captain Lionel Osborne. The 4979-ton *Llanover*, built in Sunderland in 1928, was as undistinguished as a tramp of her day could be, with a bow as straight as a cliff face, an old-fashioned counterstern, accommodation in square blocks, and a tall 'Woodbine' funnel providing natural draught for her economy-conscious Scotch boilers. She would break no records for miles steamed per day, nor would her Spartan interior raise shouts of acclaim, but she was a sound, reliable ship, well-crewed and ably commanded.

Although Captain Osborne was perhaps uneasy about his vulnerable position in the ranks of the convoy – the *Llanover* would be one of the first in the U-boats' sights in the event of an attack – he had no real fears for the Atlantic crossing. ONS 92 was a slow convoy, with a designated speed of 7½ knots, and suited the limited capability of the *Llanover*'s engines; it also had, in the combined North American force, a relatively powerful escort. Moreover, the weather was good and, being early summer, looked set to stay that way. For all that the passage would be no weekend pleasure cruise for Osborne and his crew. Two weeks of unrelieved tension and sleepless nights would take their toll. At the end of it there was the compensation of a short break in a land as yet untroubled by the hardships of war, but in the background there would always be the prospect of the homeward passage, deep-laden and doubly at risk.

It had been a long wait for Johann Mohr, Hans-Peter Hinsch and Otto Ites. At dawn on 11 May, they were still cruising aimlessly in the region of 53°N 29°W, the mid-point of the Allied convoy route across the North Atlantic. The weather continued fine, with a light easterly wind, smooth sea and good visibility. Later that morning, however, the trio's patience was at last rewarded by the sight of smoke on the eastern horizon. First one, then two, then a forest of masts and funnels came into view, silhouetted against the rising sun. Convoy ONS 92, unaware of the danger threatening, was steaming right into their trap. The U-boats submerged and prepared for the usual game of 'cat and mouse', shadowing the convoy by day and racing in to attack under the cover of darkness.

Overconfident perhaps, Mohr and his companions betrayed their presence by engaging in needless radio chatter. An alert wireless operator in the convoy's rescue ship, the British steamer *Bury*, picked up their transmissions and reported to the convoy escort commander. Later in the day the *Bury*'s report was confirmed by the Admiralty Submarine Tracking Room in London, which had intercepted and decoded positional messages from the U-boats to Lorient. It was an increasingly common failing with the U-boats that they found it difficult, or thought it unnecessary, to keep radio silence when they were in the Atlantic. For many of them it led to their eventual downfall.

Shortly after receipt of the Admiralty's warning, the convoy escort commander, in the destroyer USS *Gleaves*, took his ship, in company with the coastguard cutter USS *Spencer*, to make a visual and Asdic search right around the convoy up to a distance of 18 miles. At 1750, with the sun low in the west, *Gleaves* sighted a U-boat on the surface and gave chase. The pursuit was futile, for as soon as the American ship came within gun range the U-boat submerged. *Gleaves* continued to search with Asdic and twice made contact with the U-boat, but was unable to sink her. The hunt went on after dark with *Gleaves* and *Spencer* making broad sweeps around the convoy which, with all ships in a state of constant readiness, continued to zig-zag towards the west.

On board the *Llanover* the atmosphere was tense. Warned of

the presence of U-boats by a general signal made by the Convoy Commodore, Osborne made what preparations he could to meet the expected attack. Lifejackets were donned, all guns manned and lookouts doubled. The night, when it came, was fine and clear, perfect weather for the U-boats to do their work. Osborne was now, more than ever, acutely aware of his ship's exposed position. His fears increased when, at 2300, just as the convoy had discontinued zig-zagging, two rockets soared into the air from a ship ahead of the *Llanover* and burst in a flurry of brilliant white stars. *U-124* had opened the action.

Ringing the alarm bells was something of an irrelevance, but Osborne did it nevertheless, bringing his already alert crew to a fine pitch of readiness. He swung his binoculars in the direction of the Commodore's ship, expecting the coloured lights to flare, indicating an emergency turn, which normally followed the torpedoing of a ship in convoy. The Commodore's ship remained in darkness. Five minutes later the *Llanover* drew abeam of the torpedoed ship, which Osborne identified as the leader of his column, the 7065-ton *Empire Dell*.

As Captain Osborne was silently debating the advisability of going to the aid of the sinking ship, the lookout in the port wing of the *Llanover* shouted a warning. Swinging around, Osborne was in time to see the phosphorescent track of a torpedo speeding towards his ship from three points abaft the beam. Johann Mohr was looking for a second victim.

It was too late for Osborne to take evasive action; at the *Llanover*'s leisurely 7½ knots, even with the wheel hard over, several minutes would elapse before she even started to turn. The torpedo took her in the port quarter, squarely in her after cargo hold. The force of the explosion ripped open the half-inch steel plates of her hull as though they were so much paper and the Atlantic poured into the empty hold.

The *Llanover* lurched drunkenly to port and the steady beat of her engines accelerated to a frantic tattoo, then slowed to a shuddering halt as the main steam valve was shut by the engineer on watch. The explosion in the after hold had demolished the shaft tunnel, snapping the hardened steel shaft it protected like a brittle stick, leaving the *Llanover* without means of propulsion.

With a shrug of resignation, Osborne walked over to the big brass engine-room telegraph that had faithfully conveyed orders from the bridge to the engine-room over the years and swung the handle to 'Finished With Engines' for the last time. He prayed that, in accordance with his standing orders, the watertight door to the shaft tunnel had been closed when the alarm bells rang.

As if to protest at the cruel wound she had suffered, the *Llanover*'s steam whistle now added its voice to the confusion, filling the night with a high-pitched wail of anguish. All efforts to silence it were unsuccessful; some buckling of the funnel had jammed the steam inlet valve in the open position. Shouting above the din, Osborne ordered the Third Officer to launch the two rockets which would alert the rest of the convoy to their plight. Even this simple operation went wrong, one of the rockets exploding on ignition, severely scorching the junior officer's hand.

The *Llanover* was settling quickly by the stern and Osborne was not surprised to learn that the watertight door in the engine-room had indeed been left open. The engine spaces were flooding and had been evacuated. The situation moved from serious to desperate, but Osborne, with the ingrained loyalty of a master mariner to his ship, was reluctant to let her go. He believed she might still be saved, but he was also aware that the U-boat might at any moment put a second torpedo into her. The need to save the lives of his crew prevailed and, grudgingly, he gave the order to abandon ship. The two lifeboats were lowered without mishap and Osborne and his men left the *Llanover* unhurriedly, and without panic. Miraculously, the only casualty of the attack was the Third Officer's burned hand.

When the boats had rowed clear of the ship, Osborne was, for the first time, able to see the full extent of the damage. The whole of the *Llanover*'s poop structure had been demolished and she was visibly down by the stern, but not dangerously so. With her propeller shaft broken she could not steam under her own power, but there might be the possibility of a tow. The sea being reasonably calm, Osborne decided to wait out the night in the boats and re-board the ship next morning, assuming she was still afloat. However, an hour later the rescue ship *Bury* came looking for them, and much as he hated leaving his stricken ship, Osborne could not refuse his men the chance of safety.

Following the sinking of the *Empire Dell* and the attack on the *Llanover* by *U-124*, ONS 92 appears to have continued steaming without taking any violent evasive action. This gave the other U-boats the opportunity to move in and, an hour after the opening of the attack, Hans-Peter Hinsch, in *U-569*, fired a fan of torpedoes which, much to his chagrin, passed harmlessly between the lines of ships. Ites, in *U-94*, had better luck, sinking the 5630-ton Panama-flagged *Cocle* just after midnight. Fifteen minutes later Mohr returned to the attck, sinking in quick succession the 4371-ton Greek ship *Mount Parnes* and the British steamer *Cristales* of 5389 tons. It was only then that the Commodore ordered a series of emergency turns. These manoeuvres, combined with intense escort activity, forced the U-boats to withdraw again. Signals heard on 500 Kcs during the night indicated that the Germans were still in the vicinity, but they took no further action against the convoy.

At dawn the *Llanover* was still afloat and in sight from the deck of the *Bury*. Lionel Osborne immediately requested permission to return to his ship with a skeleton crew. The Escort Commander, no doubt understanding Osborne's feelings for his ship, agreed to a re-boarding, with the proviso that the *Llanover* was able to proceed under her own steam. Not surprisingly, Osborne could give no such guarantee, knowing in his heart that his ship would never steam again. He did, however, persuade the master of the *Bury* to turn back and close the *Llanover*. As they drew near, it became obvious that the torpedoed ship was slowly sinking and Osborne was forced to concede defeat. Three hours later he watched grim-faced as the Canadian corvette *Arvida* administered the *coup de grâce* to his ship with her 4-inch. The *Llanover* went down at 0946, almost eleven hours after being hit.

Its ranks considerably thinned, the convoy steamed on. The night of the 12th was again fine and clear, with a smooth sea, and it was no surprise when the U-boats returned soon after dark, following in the wake of the convoy on the surface. *Gleaves* and *Spencer* raced into the attack with guns and depth charges whenever the opportunity arose, and with apparent good effect. Mohr and the luckless Hinsch were driven off. Ites, however, was able to evade the escorts and at 0022 on the 13th, as the convoy was in the process of completing a prearranged 90 degree turn to port *U-94* sank the 4399-ton British ship *Batna*, and four hours later, the 4471-ton neutral *Tolken*, which flew the Swedish flag.

The convoy suffered no further attacks, but it must be said that two of the three U-boats involved had achieved considerable success. Between them they had accounted for five ships, totalling 27,414 tons, the lion's share going to Johann Mohr in *U-124*. Of the handling of ONS 92 during the forty-eight hours it was under attack some doubts must be raised. The presence of the U-boats was detected early on the morning of the 11th, some eighteen hours before the first torpedo was fired. No less than three messages were received from the Admiralty during that day warning that the convoy was being shadowed and its position being reported to Lorient by one or more enemy submarines. Yet, apart from zig-zagging around the mean course, the convoy appears to have taken no positive evasive action throughout that day and much of the following night. It was not until the fifth ship was going down, at around 0100 on the 12th, that the Commodore instituted a succession of emergency turns designed to spoil the aim of the U-boats, who were then already among the convoy. It is feasible that, had ONS 92 made a radical alteration as soon as complete darkness came on the night of the 11th, and run away from the U-boats, there might have been no ships lost. Of course, it is no mean feat of collective seamanship to put forty-one cumbersome merchant ships, sailing in close order, through a radical change of course at night without using signal lights. Nevertheless, this manoeuvre had been successfully used in convoys escorted by the Royal Navy for some time. It may be that the relatively inexperienced American escort commander of ONS 92, like many of his compatriots, preferred to perfect his own methods of anti-submarine warfare rather than adopt the well-tried British tactics.

On the afternoon of 13 May the *Bury*, which now had 143 survivors on board and was running short of food, was ordered to leave the convoy and head for St John's, Newfoundland, some 700 miles away. With her went Captain Lionel Osborne and the men of the *Llanover*. They had lost their ship, but before many weeks had elapsed they would be back at sea in a new ship and carrying on with what to them was just a job of work.

Johann Mohr and his two companions remained in the area after the passing of ONS 92, no doubt encouraged by their success. Less than a month later they were able to set up a similar ambush for Convoy ONS 100 as it sailed westward in the track of ONS 92. Once again the unlucky Hinsch failed to score a hit, but Mohr and Ites between them disposed of another five ships.

U-124 went on to sink another 44,443 tons of Allied shipping, before being destroyed off Oporto on 2 April 1943 in a combined action by the Royal Australian Navy sloop *Swan* and the British corvette *Stonecrop*. Johann Mohr perished with his crew.

14

Operation Torch

When Captain William Barnes assumed command of the 2012-ton *Garlinge* at Greenock in October 1942, he took on his shoulders a task men twice his age might have shunned. Barnes was serving as chief officer in the ship when the exigencies of war in the form of a mounting casualty list of senior officers prompted his sudden promotion to command. He was then only twenty-six years old, with the ink barely dry on his master's certificate. The *Garlinge*, on the other hand, was reaching the geriatric stage of her long life.

Built in 1918, when an earlier world war was just drawing to a close, the *Garlinge* was one of an original fleet of seven vessels owned by Constants Ltd of London, whose trade was between British and Mediterranean ports. She was a small, conventional steamship, 284 feet long, 42 feet in the beam, and in her younger days had been capable of a top speed of 10 knots. Three of her sisters had already been lost by enemy action in this present war and, as the newly-promoted Captain Barnes was all too well aware, the *Garlinge* might soon become Constants' fourth casualty. The Admiralty, in its wisdom, had chosen her to take part in the first great amphibious invasion of the war. For a ship of her size and limited capability, the risks involved in her forthcoming voyage promised to be enormous.

Operation 'Torch' was to be an assault on the North African ports of Casablanca, Algiers and Oran, using American and Canadian troops carried in British ships. In the first landings 90,000 men and their equipment were scheduled to be put ashore at three beacheads. The total invasion fleet, including escorts, was to number 340 ships, one section sailing across the Atlantic with the US contingent and the other to carry the First Canadian Division from Britain. Meticulous planning called for all ships to pass through – or in the case of the Casablanca-bound ships, close to – the Straits of Gibraltar between the night of the 5th and the morning of the 7th of November. The landings were to take place simultaneously on the morning of the 8th.

German intelligence was aware that an Allied invasion of North Africa was about to take place – this had earlier been leaked by Free French and Russian sources – but they had been unable to discover the precise location of the assault. Hitler favoured Dakar and ordered a force of forty U-boats to patrol the approaches to North-West Africa between Gibraltar and Senegal. In the western Mediterranean a smaller combined force of German and Italian U-boats was operating off North Africa as part of the normal offensive against Allied shipping. Among these modern corsairs of the Barbary Coast was Kapitänleutnant Friedrich Guggenberger in *U-81*. Guggenberger was no stranger to the area, having found fame by torpedoing and sinking the 22,600-ton British aircraft carrier *Ark Royal* near Gibraltar twelve months earlier.

When the *Garlinge* left the Clyde on 21 October, although she was to be an integral part of Operation 'Torch', her cargo of 2,700 tons of coal seemed singularly unwarlike for the operation in which she was engaged. It was as though she was considered too old and slow to be trusted with anything more than the cargo she had carried outwards from the Bristol Channel ports for so much of her life before the war. But to the young Captain Barnes and his crew their ship's role in the coming invasion was as vital as that of any of the bigger ships carrying troops and guns. Coal was a source of energy without which no invasion force of the day could survive for long. In the sandy plains of North Africa their cargo would be very much in demand.

The eight-day passage from the Clyde to Gibraltar passed without serious incident, giving Barnes a breathing space to settle in to his new command. He was fortunate to have with him as chief officer Robert Macmillan, a man thirty years his senior. The youth of Barnes and the wisdom and experience of

Macmillan provided a good basis for a happy and efficient ship at a time when the war at sea was reaching another peak. In the previous month no less than eighty-seven Allied merchant ships had been sunk by U-boats in the Atlantic.

In the closing days of October 1942, when the invasion fleets were nearing the approaches to the Mediterranean, the patrolling U-boats were, either by chance or design, drawn away to the south by the sighting of Convoy SL 125, homeward bound in ballast from Freetown. In a running battle that lasted four days and ranged from the Canaries to a position 500 miles to the west of the Straits of Gibraltar, SL 125 lost thirteen ships, but its sacrifices undoubtedly saved the heavily laden invasion fleets. While the men of SL 125 were fighting for their lives, the great armada of ships carrying the wherewithal to mount Operation 'Torch' slipped past undetected. In their midst was the small, rust-streaked collier *Garlinge*.

After a short stop at Gibraltar, the *Garlinge* left that port on the night of 7 November in company with three other merchant ships and an escort of five anti-submarine trawlers, the main invasion fleet having already sailed for Algiers. The four merchantmen set off in line abreast, with the escorting trawlers positioned ahead, astern and on either beam of the small convoy. There was none of the bustling majesty of a large Atlantic convoy, attended by destroyers and corvettes, all anxious to show off their bow waves. However, Captain William Barnes was quite happy with the arrangement. Five escorts to four merchant ships was rather more than he had been used to, even if the escorts were only old fishermen dressed up to look like men-of-war. Furthermore, in the event of attack, the *Garlinge* should be able to defend herself. She mounted a 12-pounder, four 20mm Oerlikons, two twin-Marlins and the usual array of anti-aircraft rockets. And this armament was not manned by a bunch of enthusiastic merchant seamen with only a passing knowledge of gunnery, but by a trained force thirteen DEMS gunners. Barnes was, of course, taking for granted that any attack on the convoy, if and when it came, would be from the air. In the event the first threat came from the old enemy.

It has long been an accepted myth, perpetuated by poets and, more lately, by travel agents, that the Mediterranean Sea is a placid blue lake undisturbed by the meaner side of nature. This is far from reality. From October to April depressions regularly sweep in from the Atlantic, bringing gales as fierce as any experienced in northern waters. The strongest winds usually blow from the west but on occasions when a depression passes to the south of the area, the wind direction is reversed. This was the state of affairs when the small convoy left Gibraltar on the 420-mile passage to Algiers.

Shortly after rounding Europa Point the *Garlinge* found herself steaming into the teeth of a force 6 easterly wind, which was whipping up a rough head sea. Although her ageing engine was determinedly making revolutions for 10 knots, her progress through the water was reduced to a mere crawl as she dipped her blunt bows into a sea growing steeper by the hour. Very soon, down to 5 knots, she began to drop astern of the other ships and was in danger of becoming a straggler and easy prey for the enemy. The Convoy Commodore, unwilling to lose almost a quarter of the cargo in his charge, even if it was only coal, made a number of reductions in the speed of the convoy in order that the *Garlinge* might maintain station. But by nightfall on the 9th his patience had been tried too much and, signalling the collier to proceed independently, he ordered the convoy's speed increased to 6½ knots. The labouring *Garlinge* slowly fell further and further astern until the darkness folded around her and she was lost to sight.

Phlegmatically accepting the situation as being beyond his control, Captain Barnes maintained his course and speed, determined at all cost to deliver his cargo to the Americans who were by now ashore in Algiers. As the night progressed there was no perceptible improvement in the weather, the wind remaining strong from the east and the rough sea continuing to batter the small ship with undiminished vigour. Although the visibility was good, the night was moonless and black enough for Barnes to be reasonably confident that his ship would be able to struggle along unseen by hostile eyes until daylight. He left the bridge in charge of the officer of the watch and went below to rest while the opportunity was there.

101

Chief Officer Robert Macmillan had the middle watch, from midnight to four am, on the morning of the 10th. At 0045 he estimated the position of the *Garlinge* to be 21 miles due north of Cape Ivi, a low headland backed by the massive peaks of the Atlas mountains. The port of Algiers lay some 180 miles to the east, another thirty-three hours steaming, assuming there was no moderation in the weather. Unhappily, the fate of the *Garlinge* was not to rest solely with the weather; as Macmillan plotted his position on the chart Friedrich Guggenberger was manoeuvring *U-81* into position to attack.

The torpedo struck the *Garlinge* in her port side between the engine-room and the stokehold; it was a classic U-boat strike, designed to cause the maximum damage below the waterline. The explosion of the 750lb warhead lifted the ship bodily out of the water, at the same time ripping her hull wide open. Her labouring engine stopped and a great cloud of steam and smoke shot up from her stokehold to envelop the bridge. Captain Barnes, wide awake, reached the wheelhouse within seconds of the explosion.

A hurried inspection below decks revealed the enormity of the damage. The engine-room was finished, completely wrecked, and flooding rapidly. The tall funnel, sheared off at its base, was leaning at an angle of 45 degrees, held only by its stays, while the port lifeboat had gone, reduced to matchwood by the blast. The ship had taken a pronounced port list, which was increasing with alarming rapidity. Barnes realized that the *Garlinge*, his first command, of which he had been so very proud, had very little time left afloat.

While Barnes gathered up the ship's confidential books and hurled them over the side in their weighted canvas bag, Chief Officer Macmillan mustered what crew he could find and began lowering the one remaining lifeboat. It was too late. Before the boat reached the water the *Garlinge* gave a sickening lurch and capsized. Barnes, who was still on the bridge, was dragged under with his sinking ship. Deeper and deeper he was sucked down into the black water until his lungs were on the point of bursting: then, miraculously untouched by the tangled rigging and falling wreckage, he shot to the surface. Shaking his head to clear the water from his eyes, he was relieved to see dark shape of a liferaft tossing on the waves nearby.

Fighting his way through the rough seas, Barnes reached the raft and clambered aboard, joining First Radio Officer Charles Ball, who was already clinging to the wooden slats. Clusters of tiny red lifejacket lights bobbing on the surface of the sea around the raft indicated the presence of other survivors, and Barnes and the radio officer were soon pulling other men aboard. They rescued seven who were close to the raft, but when they attempted to paddle towards lights seen further off they could make no headway against the sea.

After a while the nine men huddled together on the tiny wooden raft sighted one of the convoy's escorting trawlers and it seemed that salvation was at hand. But in spite of their cries for help and a smoke float set off by Barnes, the trawler passed by, apparently without seeing them.

Daylight came on the 10th and for the men on the pitching liferaft it brought more hope and more cruel disappointment. On two separate occasions an aircraft flew over, but took no notice of their frenzied waving and smoke floats. The morale of the already traumatized survivors sank to a new low. Five more miserable hours passed, then, just before noon, their hopes were again raised by the sight of another trawler close by. This time it was rescue. HMS *Minna*, one of the escorts, had come back for them.

The trawler first picked up five men from two other rafts floating in the vicinity and then took on Barnes and his companions. *Minna* continued the search and, four hours later, sixteen hours after the *Garlinge* had taken her sudden plunge, Chief Officer Robert Macmillan was found clinging to two wooden hatchboards and was also plucked from the sea. However, he was the last man to be found. Of the *Garlinge*'s crew of forty only fifteen had survived her sinking. Twenty-five men, including her Second Officer, Chief, Second and Third Engineers, Second Radio Officer and seven DEMS gunners had perished. For William Barnes his first voyage in command and his involvement in Operation 'Torch' had ended in outrageous bad fortune and ultimate tragedy.

103

The landing of British and American troops on the Algiers beachheads began shortly after 0100 on 8 November. There was some delay and confusion, due mainly to the inexperienced Americans landing in the wrong positions, but fortunately the opposition put up by the Vichy French was uncoordinated and far from strong. Elsewhere, at Casablanca and Oran, the story was very similar. Operation 'Torch', as a whole, was an unqualified success, and six months later led to the surrender of 240,415 German and Italian troops. The enemy's adventure in North Africa was at an end. In the initial days of 'Torch', when 90,000 Allied men and their equipment were put ashore, only one ship was lost, the unfortunate collier *Garlinge*.

Kapitänleutnant Friedrich Guggenberger reached the peak of his career with the sinking of the *Garlinge*. He was to send only five more ships to the bottom before being taken prisoner when in command of *U-513*, which was sunk by aircraft off the coast of Brazil in July 1943. After the war Guggenberger remained with the German Navy, eventually retiring with the rank of rear-admiral. *U-81* also ran out of luck with the torpedoing of the *Garlinge*. She returned to the Mediterranean in January 1943 under the command of Oberleutnant Johann Krieg, but was able to account for only two ships and a handful of small coasters, before being destroyed by Allied aircraft while alongside her berth in Pola, Yugoslavia, a year later.

15

Christmas in the South Atlantic

Of all the great oceans the South Atlantic is the most well-behaved and is regarded by seamen to be a fair weather run for much of the year. The North Atlantic is constantly swept by malicious storms summer and winter, the Indian Ocean is plagued by the miserable south-west monsoon from April to September, and even the supposedly benign Pacific feels the savage lash of the typhoon and cyclone sporadically throughout the year. North of the notorious Roaring Forties, the South Atlantic, being largely devoid of islands which can trigger drifting masses of unstable air into malevolent cyclonic disturbances, has a weather pattern that is both predictable and pleasant. It is affected only by the south-east trades, so eagerly sought after by the windjammers of yesterday. These benevolent winds, resulting from a permanent high pressure system centred over the area, blow across the ocean from the Cape of Good Hope to the Equator. They are constant in direction and rarely stronger than force 5 on the Beaufort Scale – no more than a fresh breeze to the deep-sea mariner. With them the trades bring blue skies dotted with fair-weather cumulus, and sunrises and sunsets whose beauty once seen is never forgotten. It was into these halcyon waters that the 4814-ton British steamer *Queen City* set sail in the closing days of 1942.

Commanded by Captain G. Hornsby, the *Queen City* left Cape Town on 1 December with 7,900 tons of general cargo destined for the Caribbean island of Trinidad. Her intended course followed the great circle track to a point four degrees south of the Equator, midway between the east coast of Brazil and Atol das Rocas, an island 120 miles off the mainland. From there she would follow the Brazilian coast west-north-westwards to her destination, the total distance to steam being 5,315 miles. At the 15-year-old *Queen City*'s average speed of 9¼ knots, this would be a passage of twenty-four days, culminating – or so it was hoped by all on board – in an arrival in Trinidad on Christmas Day.

For Hornsby and his crew the passage ahead had all the makings of a peacetime trans-ocean cruise, for these were waters where the drums of war were so muted as to be almost inaudible. But there were some on board who remembered the terrible mauling the *Queen City* had suffered at the hands of German bombers off Kinnaird Head in the autumn of 1940, and there was the inevitable talk of surface raiders being at sea and on the lookout for ships like their own sailing unescorted. In the past the *Admiral Graf Spee*, *Admiral Scheer* and a number of German armed merchant cruisers had passed this way, leaving in their wake a substantial string of Allied merchantmen resting on the bottom.

The reality was that the *Queen City* had little to fear from German surface raiders. The *Graf Spee* was long gone from the scene, ignominiously scuttled by her own crew off the River Plate, the *Scheer* was hiding in the Norwegian fjords and, since the sinking of the AMCs *Stier*, *Komet* and *Thor* in quick succession in the previous three months, the German Naval Staff had abandoned any further ventures in this line. The bailiwick of the South Atlantic had now passed into the hands of Admiral Dönitz who, true to form, had wasted no time in bringing in his U-boats. Long before the *Queen City* sailed from Cape Town nine German U-boats were on station off the Brazilian coast. With them was the Italian submarine *Tazzoli*, under the command of Capitano di Corvetta Carlo Fecia di Cossato. Dönitz's South Atlantic team was supported by a 'milch cow', a 1700-ton U-tanker stationed off the lonely St Paul's Rocks for refuelling.

The Italian submarines, some of which had been operating in

106

the Atlantic in conjunction with the U-boats since August 1940, had not really achieved any great success, and were, in fact, regarded by Dönitz with little more than contempt. It would seem that, as with the rest of Mussolini's fighting forces, the Italian submariners were not over-enthusiastic for their task. Conditions prevailing on board the Italian boats may have had a lot to do with this. Officers and men were strictly segregated, even to the extent of separate galleys, with a wide disparity in the food served. There is no doubt that the officers lived on the edge of luxury – if such a thing can be said to exist in a submarine at sea – while the ratings had to be content with the other end of the scale. This was in complete contrast to life in British and German submarines, where all ranks shared equally the discomforts of life under water. However, Fecia di Cossato may have been the exception that proves the rule. Although the class division aboard the *Tazzoli* was as bad as in other Italian boats, di Cossato's men worshipped him. It is probable that it was so as a result of this relationship that he had been able to sink thirteen Allied ships totalling 73,082 tons in the twenty months he had commanded the *Tazzoli*.

On the long, lonely leg of the passage from Cape Town to the Brazilian coast the *Queen City*'s wireless operators intercepted a number of transmissions indicating that U-boats were abroad in the area, but no confirmation or diversionary signals were received from the Admiralty. Following the old adage that no news is good news, Captain Hornsby continued on his planned course. The ocean was big, his ship small, and for much of the passage the probability of being sighted by a patrolling U-boat was remote. When she neared the Brazilian coast the situation would be different. Then would be the time for the *Queen City* to look to her defences. These were much the same as carried by any British merchantman at the time, a 4-inch anti-submarine gun, a high/low angle 12-pounder and four Hotchkiss machine guns. This armament was manned and maintained by six DEMS gunners.

Twenty days out of Cape Town, the *Queen City* had rounded the north-eastern bulge of South America and was steaming west-north-west at about 250 miles off the coast of Brazil. It was

107

four days before Christmas and the ship was just 890 miles from Trinidad. The weather was fine, the horizon clear and a favourable south-easterly breeze was helping her along. All was well. Then, at sunset on 21 December, she sailed into Capitano di Cossato's sights.

The first torpedo struck on the starboard side immediately under the *Queen City*'s bridge. There was a blinding flash, a deafening explosion and a huge column of water shot into the air to cascade down on those who stood transfixed on the steamer's bridge, Captain Hornsby among them. Before they had time to collect their scattered wits, a second torpedo tore into the starboard side of No. 4 hold, the explosion blowing the wooden hatch covers and tarpaulins skywards. Both starboard lifeboats were smashed by the blast.

Within a few seconds the *Queen City*, her engine-room and three of her holds open to the sea, took a heavy list to starboard. Acting quickly, for he knew he had little time, Hornsby gave the order to abandon ship. Fortunately, only a moderate sea was running and the two lifeboats on the port side were lowered without difficulty. Both boats, containing the *Queen City*'s entire crew of forty-five, all uninjured, were clear of the sinking ship seven minutes after she was first hit – a remarkable achievement.

Soon after firing her second torpedo the *Tazzoli* surfaced about a quarter of a mile off the *Queen City*'s starboard bow. Showing unusual regard for his victims, Fecia di Cossato waited until the lifeboats had rowed well out of harm's way, then manoeuvred the submarine round to the port side of the ship and opened fire with his deck gun at point blank range. The gun barked seven times, each shell finding its mark in the hull of the already crippled ship. Ten minutes after receiving the first torpedo the *Queen City* rolled upright and sank with dignity on an even keel.

Finding it hard to ignore the lump in his throat, Hornsby turned his face away from the death of his ship to run his eyes dispassionately over the submarine as it motored towards his boat. She was a sleek, newly-painted craft, well over 200 feet long he estimated, and of about 2000 tons displacement. She had

108

two deck guns, and the red, white and green flag of Italy flew at the after end of her large conning tower. Most of her crew appeared to have come on deck, perhaps to gloat over their victims. Two men, tall with very blonde hair, might have been Germans; they stood out in stark contrast to the short, dark Italians. Di Cossato was easily recognizable as the submarine's commander. Although no more than 5' 6" tall, and dressed in nondescript blue shorts and shirt, his fierce black beard and aggressive air of authority left little to doubt.

As the *Tazzoli* drew near, Hornsby steeled himself to face the second ordeal of the night. Since early in the war, it had been standard U-boat policy, whenever possible, to take prisoner the master, and sometimes the senior officers, of a torpedoed Allied ship. There was sound reasoning behind this, for, certainly as far as British ships were concerned, experienced senior men were irreplaceable, except over a long period. Hornsby considered it was his plain duty to avoid capture and, furthermore, having got his men off the *Queen City* without loss or injury, it was his firm intention to see them to the safety of the nearest land. Providentially, when the ship had been taken so rudely from under him, Hornsby was dressed, like di Cossato, in shorts and shirt with no badges of rank. In a lifeboat crowded with twenty-three men, he hoped to pass as a nobody.

When the *Tazzoli* closed Hornsby's boat, as anticipated, di Cossato called for the captain of the ship to indentify himself. Before anyone had the opportunity to give him away, Hornsby, posing as a rating, replied that the Captain was not in the boat and his whereabouts were not known. In answer to question regarding the ship's officers he gave the same reply. His act was successful, for, somewhat naively it would seem, di Cossato accepted that the boat contained only ratings and backed away. It is possible that he believed that British merchant ships were run on similar strictly segregated lines to the *Tazzoli*, resulting in all officers being in one lifeboat and ratings in another.

However, the bearded Italian met with no better success when he went alongside the other boat. This time he asked for the Chief Engineer, and was again outwitted. The *Queen City*'s chief, seeing the submarine approaching, quickly peeled off his uniform jacket and sat on it, remaining inconspicuous thereafter. A sailor in the boat took the cue and informed the Italian that the Chief Engineer had gone down with the ship. Frustrated, but determined not to leave empty-handed, Fecia di Cossato then picked one of the survivors at random – he happened to be a steward – and ordered him aboard the submarine. The commander then threw two cartons of cigarettes into the boat and made off.

Watching the *Tazzoli* motor away towards the horizon, Hornsby turned his mind to the problems of survival. The *Queen City*'s wireless transmitter had been smashed by the blast of the first torpedo and there had been no opportunity to send an SOS. Fortunately, however, the ship's lifeboat transmitter, a cumbersome affair contained in a large waterproofed suitcase – which di Cossato, for his own peace of mind, should have confiscated – was safe in the bottom of the boat and in working order. As soon as the submarine was out of sight, Hornsby instructed the wireless operator to send out a distress call, giving the position of the sinking of the *Queen City*. However, after only seven transmissions of less than two minutes each, the battery of the transmitter was found to be flat.

Realizing it was most unlikely that his call for help had been heard in such a short time, Hornsby was now faced with a life or death decision. He could keep his lifeboats drifting in roughly the same position and hope to be picked up by a passing ship or make an attempt to reach land. Had they been in more frequented waters, Hornsby would have streamed the sea anchors and waited for rescue, but this was an empty part of the ocean. On the other hand, the nearest land, the northern coast of Brazil in the region of St Luiz, lay some 200 miles to the south. This was a formidable distance for the two open boats to sail under the equatorial sun, but Hornsby concluded it was better to die in the attempt to reach land than to end up as dehydrated corpses drifting in the slough of their own hopelessness.

At 1830, after a brief consultation with Chief Officer A.H. Tarr, who was at the helm of the other boat, Hornsby ordered the sails to be hoisted and course set to the south for Brazil. Tarr's boat soon showed itself to be the better sailer and within two hours it had pulled so far ahead that Hornsby lost sight of it in the darkness.

An examination of the lockers and tanks of Hornsby's boat revealed it was well provisioned. There was a good supply of condensed milk, Horlicks tablets and pemmican, while the fresh water tanks were full. But, uncertain of how long they would take to reach the land, Hornsby prudently rationed the water to two full dippers, or about a third of a pint, per man per day. There was a fair sailing wind and, although the ungainly boat's speed was no more than 4 knots at the best, progress was steady and in the right direction. The nights were blessedly cool, but the days, with the sun almost directly overhead, were unbearably hot. Most of the survivors were clad only in shorts and shirt and, as there was very little shade in the boat, they suffered the agonies of sunburn. In spite of this, the morale of the men was good.

At about 2100 on the night of 23 December, after sailing steadily for only two days and two nights, the lights of the shore were sighted. Hornsby approached the land warily and, after judging the breakers to be too big for a safe landing at night, decided to stand off until daylight. Setting sail again at dawn, the boat eventually grounded on a shelving beach at four o'clock that afternoon. It was Christmas Eve.

Discovering they had landed at Guimaraes, a small fishing village 35 miles to the west of the port of St Luiz, Hornsby's first action after stepping ashore was to find a telephone and contact the British Consul at St Luiz. Transportation by land in this remote corner of Brazil being impracticable, the Consul agreed to send a tug to pick up the survivors. Late that same afternoon Hornsby and his men reboarded their lifeboat and were towed to St Luiz, where they arrived on the morning of 25 December. It was one Christmas Day none of them would ever forget.

The *Queen City*'s second lifeboat, commanded by Chief Officer Tarr, had not fared so well. Although it had appeared to be the faster of the two boats, it had in fact made considerable leeway on its 240-mile passage. Tarr and his crew spent their Christmas at sea, finally coming ashore on an even more remote beach 58 miles to the east of St Luiz. They were fortunate enough

111

to find a spring of fresh water after landing and lived a reasonably comfortable Robinson Crusoe-like existence for two days before they managed to contact St Luiz through some local fishermen. The same tug sent to rescue their shipmates towed them into St Luiz on the 28th.

The subsequent career of Fecia di Cossato and the *Tazzoli* was short and unfruitful. The Italian submarine sank only one more merchantman before being destroyed by a British aircraft in the Bay of Biscay on 16 May 1943.

16

The Long Voyage
to Nowhere

January 1943 was a bonus month for British shipping, with only eighteen ships lost through enemy action, totalling a mere 91,056 tons. This was an immense improvement on the previous year, which had seen a consistent monthly loss of around fifty ships of 250,000 tons. Tentatively, the question being asked was, 'Is this the turning of the tide, the long-awaited emergence from darkness into light?'

The month was drawing to a close as the British ship *Llanashe* left the Iraqi port of Basrah and began her long, tortuous passage down the Shatt al Arab river to the sea. Homeward bound to the United Kingdom, she had ahead of her a voyage of 6000 miles, during which she would be the potential prey of German and Japanese submarines and an unknown number of enemy surface raiders. With a maximum speed of 9½ knots and an armament consisting of a 4.7-inch and four light machine guns, she was odds-on favourite for extinction.

The *Llanashe* was one of the newer ships in the fleet of Evan Thomas, Radcliffe. Built in 1936 by Bartram & Son of Sunderland, she was of 4836 tons gross and, while no ocean greyhound, she had pleasing lines for a tramp ship of her day. In her short life before the war she had carried coal from the mines of South Wales to all corners of the globe, returning, often after many months, laden with grain, ore, sugar, or whatever the charter market had to offer. In short, the *Llanashe* was a no-frills moneymaker, owned and manned by men who knew well the hard business of the sea. Her commander, Captain James Parry, was typical of that breed. But, experienced seaman though he was, to Parry, as he paced the bridge as his ship slid past the muddy banks of the Shatt al Arab – which was to be the focus of another bloody war forty years later – the long voyage ahead must have been a daunting prospect. For more than four years he had walked the slippery tightrope of war at sea. How much longer, he wondered, would his luck hold out.

The *Llanashe*'s current cargo was unlikely to increase Parry's confidence in the future. She carried 3,500 tons of tinplate which, stowing at only 15 cubic feet to the ton, was a deadweight cargo in every sense of the word. Should her hull be breached, the *Llanashe* would go to the bottom in minutes like the proverbial stone – and Parry was well aware that the likelihood of such a disaster happening must be a probability. Prior to sailing from Basrah, he had learned that the German surface raider *Michel* was at large in the Indian Ocean and had sunk five Allied ships in the closing months of 1942. And there was also the invisible threat of attack from under the sea. At any one time there were known to be at least seven German and eight Japanese submarines operating in this area. These appeared to be hunting mainly in the approaches to the Persian Gulf and at the southern end of the Mozambique Channel, and Parry was prepared to meet the danger they posed to his ship. Fortunately, perhaps, for his peace of mind, he was not aware that five of Admiral Dönitz's new 'U-cruisers', each with a range of 30,000 miles, had recently broken into the Indian Ocean and were creating havoc among shipping rounding the Cape of Good Hope. One of their number was *U-182*, under the command of Korvettenkapitän Nicolai Clausen. James Parry and Clausen were soon to meet, but not face-to-face in this world.

For two days the *Llanashe* steamed south through the Persian Gulf with the temperature steadily climbing, much to the delight of all on board. Basrah in January was a cold, cheerless place. Off Bandar Abbas, Iran's port at the southern end of the Gulf, the *Llanashe* joined up with a small convoy which was to take her through the Strait of Hormuz and clear of the dangerous sector of the Arabian Sea where the U-boats were in the habit of setting up an ambush. Three days out of Bandar Abbas, with the Gulf of Oman astern, and abeam of Masira island, she left the convoy and set out alone on the long haul to the Cape.

The direct route from the Persian Gulf to South Africa passes close to the lonely, forbidding island of Socotra and south through the Mozambique Channel, which separates Madagascar from the African mainland. It is a distance of some 4,500 miles. In more normal times the *Llanashe* would have taken this route, rubbing shoulders with the elite cargo liners trading to the Indian sub-continent, but these were, of course, far from normal times. In the early summer of 1942 Japanese submarines congregating in the southern approaches to the Mozambique Channel had in two months sunk twenty-four ships, totalling 127,261 tons. This was an unforseen massacre that rocked the Admiralty back on their heels and sent them scurrying to their charts, seeking a safer route to and from the Cape. As a consequence, Captain Parry now laid his courses in a wide parabola, first to the south-east to pass between the Chagos Achipelago and the Seychelles, then south to Rodrigues Island, south-west to a point 300 miles clear of the southern tip of Madagascar, and so to the Cape of Good Hope. This diversion added more than 800 miles to the passage – an extra three or four days' steaming for the *Llanashe* – but it was a precaution Parry could not afford to ignore.

Crossing the Equator early in February, the *Llanashe* moved into the largely deserted waters of the South Indian Ocean. For the time being the immediate threat of attack by U-boats was past, but Parry dare not relax his vigilance. Zig-zagging by day and holding a straight course at night, he pushed the ship southwards at her maximum 9½ knots. By the 16th she was clear of the danger area off the Mozambique Channel and heading south-west for the Cape. Late that evening a wireless message was received from the Admiralty directing her to proceed to Port Elizabeth and there join a convoy for Cape Town. The distance between these two ports being a mere 420 miles, it must have been obvious to Parry that U-boats were now active off the Cape.

That night, at 2200, the *Llanashe* came around onto a more westerly course, heading for Port Elizabeth and the shelter of the convoy escorts – such as they were in this remote sphere of the war. The Cape summer had now taken an unusual turn and it was blowing a near-gale from the north, with a rough, confused sea. The night was black, the sky clear and the visibility excellent. Conditions could not have been better for Nicolai Clausen, who was lying in wait with his torpedo tubes loaded. The *Llanashe* was only 170 miles to the east of Port Elizabeth when, at 0245 on the morning of the 17th, Clausen struck.

The torpedo caught the British ship in a vulnerable spot, just abaft the engine-room. Chief Officer Samuel Lloyd, who was enjoying his last hour of fitful sleep before taking up his watch at 0400, was awoken by a dull thud. Automatically, he rolled out of his bunk and struggled into his lifejacket. When he reached the deck he realized at once that his ship had received a fatal blow. No 4 hold, immediately aft of the engine-room, was wide open to the night, its tarpaulins, hatchboards and steel beams having been blown skywards by the force of the explosion. One heavy tarpaulin, 800 square feet of canvas, was caught on the truck of the mainmast and nosily thrashing itself into shreds in the wind like a gigantic storm ensign.

The steady beat of the *Llanashe*'s engine was stilled and she appeared to be settling rapidly by the stern. All the signs were that the torpedo had hit near the watertight bulkhead separating the engine spaces from No. 4 hold and the sea was flooding into both these huge compartments. As Lloyd took in the full horror of the situation, the order came from the bridge to abandon ship and he ran for the boat deck to supervise the lowering of his boat. The *Llanashe* carried four lifeboats, two on each side of the vessel, giving ample capacity for her 42-man crew. All the boats were fitted with skates, wrap-around fenders to protect them from damage by the ship's side when being lowered in a seaway.

On this wild night the sea was running high and, although Lloyd succeeded in lowering his boat to the water without damage, as soon as it hit the waves it began to slam heavily against the ship's side. In spite of the protective skates wood splintered on steel, and Lloyd realized that unless the boat was cast off quickly it would be pounded to pieces in a matter of minutes. Showing considerable courage, he grasped one of the lifelines rigged between the davits and launched himself outwards, sliding down the rope as he went. It was his intention to cut the boat free before it was damaged beyond use. Unfortunately, as he neared the boat it was lifted on a wave and sheered away from the ship's side. Lloyd made a desperate jump for the boat, but missed and plunged into the water between the boat and the ship.

In February, which is the southern summer, the sea off the coast of South Africa is comparatively warm, averaging around 70° F, but the water felt anything but inviting to Samuel Lloyd. On this night when the world had fallen about his ears the sea was like a cold shroud which enveloped him and dragged him down. He kicked out desperately, fighting his way to the surface. When his head finally broke water, he found himself alone in a hostile sea. The lifeboat had disappeared, smashed and sunk, or swept away by the angry sea. There were no comforting voices borne on the wind, no bobbing lights to show that there were others in the water, nothing but a dull red glow emanating from the dying *Llanashe* as, weighed down by her cargo of tinplate, she slid beneath the waves stern first.

After about forty-five minutes in the water Lloyd was aware of a dark shape drifting close by, rising and falling on the waves. He swam towards it to find it was a small wooden liferaft floating perilously low in the water. Heaving himself aboard, he found the raft already occupied. The *Llanashe*'s second officer, Robert Bressey, her Japanese-born chief steward, Suetaka Saito, and the DEMS gunlayer, Hodder, were clinging to the boards of the tiny craft. They were all alive, but wet, miserable and exhausted. Lloyd's arrival on the raft did nothing to improve their situation.

What had been a near-gale viewed from the deck of the *Llanashe* was a full-blown storm down at sea level. The wind screamed and green-crested waves broke over the tossing raft, constantly threatening to tear the four survivors from their precarious perch. The thought crossed Lloyd's mind that he might have been better off going down with the ship, for his chances of survival now seemed very slim indeed. As far as he could remember from the chart, they were at least 80 miles from

117

the nearest land; other ships did come this way, but they were infrequent, and, in any case, the possibility of their half-submerged raft being sighted in this sea was not worth contemplating. To make matters worse, the fierce northerly wind was relentlessly pushing them south into the empty wastes of the great Southern Ocean, where nothing but the giant albatross and the iceberg moved. There had been no opportunity to send out an SOS before the ship went down, so there could be no hope of assistance from the shore, where their plight was, as yet, unknown. Only when the *Llanashe* was days, perhaps weeks, overdue would a search be organized. Under the conditions prevailing, any help that eventually came must be too late.

Lloyd had been some ten minutes on the liferaft when *U-182* surfaced to verify her kill. He watched fascinated as the submarine neared the raft. She was very large, with two guns on deck, one forward and one aft. Her square-shaped conning tower was crowded with men wearing heavy duffle-type coats. Obviously, as many of *U-182*'s crew as possible had come on decks to witness the results of their night's work.

The raft bumped alongside the submarine's casing, bringing Samuel Lloyd to his first and only meeting with the man responsible for his predicament, Korvettenkapitän Nicolai Clausen. Leaning over the fore end of *U-182*'s conning tower, Clausen cupped his hands and called to the men on the raft below, demanding to know the name and destination of their ship. Lloyd, who, with the *Llanashe* on the bottom and his own future in jeopardy, could see no virtue in being a silent hero, answered truthfully. It was unfortunate that Clausen's English was limited and he was completely baffled by Lloyd's strong Welsh accent. For several minutes the two men, bawling above the noise of the wind and waves, held a nonsensical shouting match that would have been hilarious in any other circumstances. It is not certain whether Clausen gained the information he required, but he eventually gave up, backed the submarine away and made off at speed, leaving the men on the raft to their fate.

It may be that Clausen's frustration swamped his more humane feelings for, in retrospect, it is hard to understand why he offered no help to the four survivors, who were so obviously in a desperate state. Given that he was unable to take them on board the U-boat, a small supply of food and water passed down to the men would have been a gesture of mercy which, as it transpired, might have made all the difference between life and death for many in the days to follow.

For Lloyd and his companions the remainder of the night was a half-remembered dream of abject misery. Then the new day dawned at last and with it came a ray of hope. Three more of the *Llanashe*'s liferafts were in sight on the heaving sea, all carrying survivors. With great difficulty the four rafts were brought together and lashed. They contained, in all, sixteen survivors, among them Chief Engineer David Harries, Second Radio Officer R. Thompson and a DEMS gunner named Woodrow. They were, it appeared, all that remained of the *Llanashe*'s crew of forty-two.

Lloyd, being the senior deck officer, took charge, determined to make the best of a bad situation. He distributed the men as comfortably as possible on the rafts and then took stock of the provisions available. Each raft was equipped with watertight tanks, which should have contained standard lifeboat rations and fresh water sufficient to keep its occupants alive for a number of days. To their horror, the survivors discovered that the tanks of three rafts were completely empty, while those on the fourth yielded only one tin of Horlicks tablets, two tins of chocolate and half a gallon of water. The thieves of the Basrah dockside had been at work.

The flame of hope kindled by the coming together of the liferafts dimmed and all but died. But there was worse to come. In the next twenty-four hours the weather deteriorated further and the overcrowded rafts were frequently capsized. Although the sea was comparatively warm, the continuing struggle to stay aboard the rafts began to take its toll. It was discovered that the Horlicks tablets, which should have given the men the energy to fight, served only to increase their thirst, and those remaining were, reluctantly, consigned to the deep. Lloyd then set the rations at one piece of chocolate and half a dipper of water each per day. To men already suffering from shock and exposure such

119

deprivation was sufficient to destroy any morale they had left.

The waterlogged flotilla of small wooden craft, battered by the wind and waves, drifted aimlessly. For their occupants there was no shelter from the burning sun by day and only cold and dampness at night. The rafts slid from crest to trough, rolling horribly without let-up and, with the exception of Lloyd and the DEMS gunlayer, Hodder, one by one the others succumbed to an awful wretching seasickness. This sickness – a malady only those who have suffered can appreciate – combined with the extremes of temperatures and lack of sustenance so weakened the survivors that they became light-headed and without hope. Ironically, the sea around them teemed with fish, but without hooks and lines to catch them, these might just as well been part of some cruel mirage. The odd flying fish that flopped aboard was immediately torn apart and eaten raw, but there were too few of these to tip the scales.

For one brief, ecstatic moment hopes of rescue ran high when an aircraft was seen flying low over the water. But the plane flew away without approaching the rafts and the survivors sank into a new trough of despondency.

Lloyd and Hodder, who seemed to be able to draw on each other's strength, worked hard to stem the tide of despair threatening to engulf the drifting rafts. They worked in vain. The others were too far gone to be chivvied into fighting for their lives. On the fifth day after the sinking of the *Llanashe* Second Officer Robert Bressey went quietly mad and died.

By the ninth day the rafts had broken adrift and there was neither the will nor the strength to bring them together again. Lloyd, Hodder and Suetaka Saito were once more alone on the wide, unfriendly ocean. All three were desperately weak and Saito, the Japanese chief steward, rambling and obviously near to death. Lloyd and Hodder, determined to live at all costs, resorted to an elaborate fantasy, plying each other with imaginary plates of steaming food and glasses of ice-cold beer. For them, the illusion worked, but Saito was beyond such childish guile. On the morning of the tenth day he was found to be dead and his body was slipped over the side. Twenty-four hours later the last of the meagre rations were eaten and Lloyd and Hodder, finally accepting the inevitable, crouched on the heaving raft, awaiting the oblivion of death.

Late on 27 February the British motor vessel *Tarrakan*, manned by a Dutch crew, was approaching Port Elizabeth from the east, intent on joining a Cape Town-bound convoy. For some reason, possibly because it was a black and stormy night, the master of the *Tarrakan* decided against entering Algoa Bay in the darkness. After sighting the lights of the port, he steamed back out to sea to await daylight.

Nest morning, as the first rays of the sun were exploring the eastern horizon, a keen-eyed lookout on the *Tarrakan* sighted three liferafts rising and falling on the long rollers. From two of the rafts the Dutchmen picked up only bodies, but on the third there was life. Chief Officer Samuel Lloyd and Gunlayer Hodder, unconscious, their emaciated bodies covered with salt water sores, were gently lifted into a cargo net and hoisted aboard the *Tarrakan*. They were landed at Cape Town on 4 March, where they spent seven weeks in hospital recovering from their terrible ordeal.

Eleven other survivors of the sinking of the *Llanashe* were rescued from a lifeboat off the fishing village of Knysna, having been carried a distance of 260 miles by the Agulhas Current, which sweeps westwards around the Cape. Of the ship's total crew of forty-two, twenty-nine had perished, including Captain James Parry, whose luck had finally run out.

Nicolai Clausen outlived James Parry by only three months. Following the despatch of the *Llanashe*, Clausen embarked on a long and unrewarding patrol off the Mozambique Channel, sinking only one ship in two months. He then returned to the North Atlantic, where, on 16 May 1943, *U-182* was caught while harassing a convoy and destroyed by the American escort vessel *Mackenzie*. Clausen and all his men went down with their boat.

17

The Last Great Battle

In mid-January 1943 Churchill and Roosevelt had one of their rare face-to-face meetings. The venue was Casablanca; the subject the invasion of enemy territory in Europe by a joint Anglo-American force. In Russia the German Sixth Army was frozen into immobility before Stalingrad and threatened with extinction, while in North Africa Rommel was caught in the jaws of a pincer movement set up by Montgomery and Eisenhower. The time was ripe for the opening of the 'Second Front' Stalin had been urging for so long. At Casablanca it was agreed to tackle Sicily and Italy first, and then the massive assault across the English Channel, probably in the late spring of 1944. However, before any move was made back into Europe, it was first necessary to transport across the North Atlantic a vast American army, together with its guns, tanks, planes and stores.

The task was a daunting one, for the battle for the Atlantic sea lanes was then rapidly moving towards a new climax. Dönitz had thrown more than 100 U-boats into the fray, most of them to hunt in packs in the 'air gap' in mid-Atlantic, where no air cover could yet be provided for convoys by the long-range Liberators and Sunderlands based on opposite sides of the ocean. If January had been an encouraging month for Allied shipping, then February was traumatic. A total of sixty-three merchant ships of 360,000 tons were sunk in this month. March was to be even worse. But if the invasion of Europe was to be a reality, there was no alternative but to increase the numbers of ships crossing the Atlantic from west to east.

In the last week of February and the first week of March, four consecutive eastbound convoys set out from New York. They involved a total of 193 Allied merchant ships and thirty-eight escort vessels. Each convoy was heavily attacked in mid-Atlantic, it being estimated that as many as seventy U-boats operated against them. In all thirty-eight merchantmen and one escorting destroyer were sunk for the loss of only one U-boat. It was an undisputed victory for Admiral Dönitz.

The fiercest sea action of all, greater in magnitude even than Trafalgar, and the last great engagement of the Battle of the Atlantic, took place from 16 to 19 March, when two eastbound convoys merged in latitude 52° N, midway between Newfoundland and Ireland. In those three momentous days, ninety merchant ships, protected by twenty escorts, fought a pitched battle with forty plus U-boats. The weather during the battle was at its North Atlantic worst, being a malignant blend of mountainous seas, fog and snowstorms, with the additional threat of drifting icebergs.

Convoy SC 122 sailed from New York on 5 March and consisted of an armada of fifty merchant ships steaming in thirteen columns abreast. US Navy ships escorted the convoy as far as the Grand Banks of Newfoundland where, on the 12th, the ocean escort took over for the passage across the open Atlantic. This group was a combined Anglo-American force commanded by Commander R.C. Boyle, RN, and consisted of the destroyers HMS *Havelock* and USS *Upshur*, the frigate HMS *Swale*, the Flower-class corvettes *Buttercup*, *Godetia*, *Lavender*, *Pimpernel* and *Saxifrage*, and the American armed trawler *Campobello*. Convoy SC 122, as indicated by its prefix, was a slow convoy, destined – God and the enemy willing – to make its way across the Atlantic at a speed of 7½ to 8 knots.

Three days after the departure of SC 122 a second convoy of forty ships, designated HX 229, slipped past the Ambrose Light and formed up in eleven columns in sight of the low foreshore of Long Island. HX 229, a 'fast' convoy, was scheduled to make the ocean crossing at 10 knots and to overtake SC 122 when both convoys were within 200 miles of the west coast of Ireland and under the full protection of the Royal Navy and RAF Coastal Command. HX 229 was joined on the 14th by its ocean

123

escort, the destroyers HMS *Volunteer, Beverley, Witherington* and *Mansfield*, and the Flower-class corvettes *Anemone* and *Pennywort*.

In the ranks of SC 122, sailing from New York on the 5th, was another of Evan Thomas, Radcliffe's ships, the *Clarissa Radcliffe*, commanded by Captain Stuart Gordon Finnes. Built in 1915 by Craig, Taylor & Company at Stockton-on-Tees, the 5754-ton *Clarissa Radcliffe*, like so many of her kind, had seen her best days. In her prime her 470 nhp engine had given her a sea speed of 10 knots but, twenty-eight years on, she would be hard pressed to maintain even the minimum of 7½ knots proposed for the convoy. On this voyage the veteran ship was loaded to her winter marks with a full cargo of iron ore, which would further handicap her from the moment she left New York harbour. For Captain Finnes and his 52-man crew facing the two-fold danger of a North Atlantic winter and the determination of the U-boats, the immediate future was full of foreboding.

Less than thirty-six hours out of New York, shortly after clearing the shelter of the Cape Cod peninsula, SC 122 ran into the full fury of a force 10 storm, which quickly turned its orderly columns into a chaos of fifty underpowered, overloaded merchantmen desperately fighting to remain afloat and on course. Within a few hours the convoy had scattered over a wide area, with each ship hidden from the other by the driving rain, and each waging its own lonely battle against the enraged elements.

The *Clarissa Radcliffe*, rolling violently through the great weight of ore low down in her holds, shipping green seas overall, and barely able to maintain steerage way, soon fell astern, and lost all contact with the rest of the convoy. Two days after the storm had passed, on 9 March, she was sighted by the Canadian corvette *The Pas*, which was returning to Halifax. The commander of *The Pas* advised Captain Finnes that his ship was only 15 miles astern of the convoy and urged him to make every effort to rejoin. With her tall funnel pouring black smoke, and her elderly engine labouring diligently, the *Clarissa Radcliffe* pressed ahead at her best speed. Only those on her bridge knew how slim were her chances of regaining contact with SC 122.

124

While SC 122 had been wrestling with the storm, the Atlantic to the eastwards was becoming a vast, shifting battleground. Fifteen hundred miles to the north-east, and in even worse weather, Convoy SC 121, which had left New York ten days earlier, was under heavy attack. German intelligence had detected the sailing and proposed route of this convoy some four days earlier, with the result that Dönitz had set up an ambush with twenty-six U-boats in the path of the ships. The attack began on the 6th and became a five-day nightmare played out in storm-force winds accompanied by snow, rain, hail and the inevitable mountainous seas. SC 121 was initially escorted by only a small force consisting of two American destroyers and three corvettes, one British and two Canadian. Air cover and more surface escorts were thrown in on the 9th when the running battle had moved to within 400 miles of the west coast of Ireland. But it was then too late. SC 121 had already lost thirteen ships of 60,000 tons to the U-boats.

No sooner had the battle for SC 121 been broken off than, 500 miles to the south-west and directly in the path of the oncoming SC 122, the fast convoy HX 228 also came under attack. Sighted on the morning of the 10th, the forty-four ship convoy suffered its first casualty that night. Over the following forty-eight hours a force of twelve to fourteen U-boats kept up a running attack, but with only limited success. Four merchant ships were sunk and the destroyer HMS *Harvester* lost. On the credit side for HX 228, the U-boat which had torpedoed the *Harvester* was rammed and sunk by the Free French corvette *Aconit*.

Late on the 14th Admiral Dönitz became aware of the huge armada of 110 ships crawling eastwards across the North Atlantic in two separate groups. SC 122 was by now 600 miles to the east of Newfoundland, with HX 229 only 300 miles astern and slowly closing the gap. German intelligence had intercepted and decoded messages from the commodores of both convoys giving exact details of ships, escorts, speed and intentions. Dönitz at once called in forty more U-boats, many of them fresh from the attacks on SC 121 and HX 228, and formed them up in the path of the two approaching convoys.

The attack on HX 229 opened on the night of the 16th/17th with the sinking of two merchant ships in the first hour. By the early hours of the 17th, HX 229, forging ahead at all speed, had caught up with and merged with SC 122. The two convoys now formed a great fleet of slow-moving shipping, wallowing in heavy seas, thinly protected by escorts and surrounded by marauding U-boats. In all 150 vessels, above and below the sea, were to be involved in the ensuing conflict.

The visibility was good and further enhanced by bright moonlight and the Northern Lights. The U-boats were, therefore, able to move in on the surface with impunity. Under such ideal conditions, and with an abundance of slow-moving targets, absolute slaughter was prevented only by the magnificent work of the convoy escorts, which were outnumbered two to one by the U-boats. In the hours remaining until dawn only five merchantmen were sunk and five others damaged.

With the coming of full daylight on the 17th the U-boat commanders seemed so confident of their impending victory that they continued to attack on the surface. They were in the 'air gap' and, so they thought, safe from retaliation by long-range bombers. But at noon on that day, much to their great surprise, a lone Liberator of Coastal Command, flying at the extreme limit of its range, appeared over the convoy and began scattering depth charges. Fearing the aircraft might be the first of many to come, the U-boats were forced to submerge. The Liberator, being 900 miles out from its base in Northern Ireland, was able to spend only a few minutes over the convoy, but there can be little doubt that its gallant effort was a severe setback to the U-boats, who had been intent on a day's uninterrupted hunting. As it was, nine more Allied ships were to go to the bottom that day.

Dönitz finally withdrew his wolf-packs on the night of the 19th, when the convoys had moved to within 450 miles of the Irish coast and Coastal Command was able to provide almost continuous air cover. At the final reckoning SC 122 had lost eight of its merchant ships and the armed trawler *Campobello*, the latter foundering in heavy seas. HX 229 suffered worse, losing thirteen ships. On the other side, one U-boat had been

126

sunk by Coastal Command and the escorts claimed seven others damaged. It was hardly a victory for the Allies, but the blood bath had at least been contained.

One ship was still missing from SC 122. This was the *Clarissa Radcliffe*, last seen straggling 15 miles astern of the convoy on 9 March. Lieutenant-Commander Old, of HMCS *The Pas*, had given the straggler the position of the convoy, and had observed her making the attempt to catch up. What happened to the *Clarissa Radcliffe* after that must remain for all time a matter of conjecture, although two possible explanations were put forward.

On the afternoon of 9 March Oberleutnant Max Kruschka, in *U-621*, claimed to have sighted a ship of about 6000 tons stopped and drifting in position 53° 15' N 41° 05' W. Kruschka fired eight torpedoes at the ship, scoring two hits. The unknown vessel did not sink. Continuing his patrol, Kruschka sighted the same ship, still afloat, on several occasions, but as she was very low in the water and apparently sinking, he was reluctant to use up any more of his precious stock of torpedoes. He finally watched the ship go down on the morning of the 12th. Researchers have since claimed that the ship was the *Clarissa Radcliffe*, but the evidence does not stand up to serious examination. The position of the attack given by Kruschka was more than 1000 miles to the north-east of the position given for the *Clarissa Radcliffe* by HMCS *The Pas* on the morning of the 9th. That Kruschka did sight and torpedo a ship on the 9th, and then watched that same ship sink three days later, is beyond dispute. However, that ship has never been identified, but it seems certain that she was not the *Clarissa Radcliffe*.

Another unidentified cargo ship was reported sighted on the 18th by Kapitänleutnant Henrich Schmid in *U-633*. This ship, again of about 6000 tons, was on an easterly course in position 52° 20' N 27° 10' W. Schmid missed with his first salvo of three torpedoes, but scored a hit with a fourth fired singly. The merchant ship sank, apparently with all hands. No Allied ship was reported lost in this area, but it seems highly unlikely that Schmid fired at a ghost. In the end, the credit for the sinking of the *Clarissa Radcliffe* was finally given to *U-633*, but in a revised position of 42° 00' N 62° 00' W. This further confuses the issue, for that position is 1,500 miles to the south-west of the one given by Schmid himself when reporting his success, and is, in fact, very near to the spot where the *Clarissa Radcliffe* was last seen by corvette *The Pas*. Unless the British ship had been hove-to for nine days, which seems most unlikely, or Heinrich Schmid's navigation was 1,500 miles in error – again unlikely – the officially recorded graveyard of the *Clarissa Radcliffe* can hardly be correct.

It seems much more likely that Captain Finnes, realizing the impossibility of catching up with the convoy, decided to proceed independently, following the shortest route to his destination. If this is indeed true, then the *Clarissa Radcliffe*, torpedoed by *U-633* on the afternoon of the 18th, probably sank only 70 miles or so to the south of where the convoy battle was raging. She was, therefore, also a casualty – albeit a lonely one – of the last great action of the Battle of the Atlantic. Whether Captain Stuart Finnes and his fifty-four men went down with their ship or died later in the lifeboats will never be known. The only apparent witnesses to the sinking, Heinrich Schmid and the crew of *U-633*, were themselves lost in the Bay of Biscay some seven weeks later when *U-633* was bombed and sunk by a British aircraft.

18

The Lone Survivor

On 7 May 1943 a small Indian dhow, her varnished hull peeling through long exposure to sun and salt water, rounded Cape Paman and glided into Mikindani Bay, a hook-shaped indent in the coast of Tanganyika. When the dhow brought up to her anchor she was forty-seven days out from India's Malabar Coast, having sailed almost 3000 miles using the dying winds of the north-east monsoon. Among the ten men on her deck was one who, although tanned a deep brown by the tropical sun, stood out from the others. He was unmistakably European.

Seven weeks earlier, on 18 March, the 7132-ton *Fort Mumford* had sailed from Colombo, bound for Aden, 2,100 miles to the west. She was carrying a cargo of military stores, including boxed aircraft on deck, a cargo which had already crossed two other oceans, and was consigned to the Mediterranean, where the return of the Allies to Europe was afoot.

Owned by the Ministry of War Transport, and managed by the Reardon Smith Line, the *Fort Mumford* was a wartime replacement ship built in Canada. She carried a crew of fifty-three, which included five DEMS gunners and one Merchant Navy gunner. Like all her sister ships of the Fort-class, she was a strictly functional, mass-produced ship with an all-welded hull, a standard triple-expansion steam engine of 505 nominal horse-power – which left her underpowered for her size – and cramped accommodation lacking any of the niceties found in most company-built ships. However, for Captain John Reardon Smith she was a considerable improvement on his previous command, which had been built in the year the *Titanic* made her first and last voyage.

John Reardon Smith, a nephew of the founder of the Reardon Smith Line, had taken his share of knocks in the war and had suffered great personal tragedy. In December 1940 he had lost his youngest son, an apprentice in the *Victoria City*, sunk in the massacre of Convoy HX 90 off Bloody Foreland. Less than eighteen months later, Reardon Smith himself had narrowly escaped death when his command, the *Botavon*, was torpedoed and sunk by a German aircraft off Murmansk with the loss of twenty-one lives.

The *Fort Mumford*'s voyage – her first – had begun in Montreal on 5 January 1943, when she was accepted from the builders by Reardon Smith and his men. A 7000-mile ballast passage to Vancouver via the Panama Canal followed, during which the new ship and her crew learned to live with each other. Her working life began in Vancouver, where she loaded a part cargo in the depths of the British Columbian winter. Not a man aboard her had any regrets when hatches were finally battened down, and the *Fort Mumford* set off on the long leg across the Pacific to Lyttelton in the south island of New Zealand.

In New Zealand they found a paradise which seemed light years removed from the war. The South Pacific summer, the magnificent scenery and, above all, the overwhelming hospitality of the people of Lyttelton made the visit as memorable as any experienced by the seamen of Captain Cook's day. For some, the temptations proved too much. Worn down by the stress of seagoing in wartime and dazzled by the contrast this new world presented to a drab, austere Britain, four of the *Fort Mumford*'s crew deserted before the ship left Lyttelton. And who could condemn them for this?

The month-long passage around the under-belly of Australia and across the Indian Ocean was trouble-free, and for Reardon Smith and the older men aboard reminiscent of those days of peace when their only enemy was the sea itself. A few hours at a buoy in Colombo harbour taking on bunkers and then, on the morning of 18 March, the *Fort Mumford* slipped out of the breakwaters and turned her bows westwards. Reardon Smith had been advised before sailing that any U-boats at large in the Arabian Sea were likely to be concentrated off Cape Guardifui, near to the eastern approaches to the Gulf of Aden. He therefore looked forward to at least another week of trouble-free steaming.

With her darkened presence betrayed only by the phosphorescence of her bow wave, the *Fort Mumford* steamed past Cape Comorin, the southernmost point of India, on the night of the 19th, and altered on to a west-north-westerly course. She was bound through the Nine Degree Channel, the wide gap between the Maldive and Laccadive Islands, which straddle the way to the east like a broken string of pearls. On the other side of the islands lay the Arabian Sea, once a bloody battleground of pirates and East Indiamen, and now host only to the leisurely sailing dhow and the occasional scurrying grey-painted merchantman.

Sunset on the 20th saw the *Fort Mumford* 90 miles due west of Suheli Par, the southernmost islet of the Laccadives. She was steaming at 9 knots through a flat calm sea, with no breath of wind, other than that she was making, to flush out the stifling heat of the day from her accommodation. With the coming of dusk, hazy conditions closed in, restricting visibility, but the officer of the watch on her bridge was not over-concerned. Very little traffic was expected in this area.

An hour later, below decks, Seaman Gunner Horace Bailey lay on top of his bunk in the cabin he shared with two of the DEMS gunners. The room was unbearably hot and Bailey heaved a sigh of relief when the other men gathered up their gear and made for the door. It was a little before eight o'clock, time to change the watch.

In the opinion of Toshiaki Fukumura, commander of the Japanese submarine *I-27*, the patrol to date had been an abject failure. Days of combing the Arabian Sea, on the surface at night and submerged by day, had revealed nothing more than a few native dhows heading south under full sail. Disappointment and frustration were consuming him, but he feared most the loss of face he would suffer if he returned to Japan with his torpedoes unused. Then, shortly before 2000 on 20 March, Fukumura's luck changed. Out of the hazy darkness loomed a large merchant ship, loaded to her marks and with her decks piled high with cargo.

Fukumura's torpedo ploughed into the *Fort Mumford* as the last stroke of eight bells rang out from her bridge. Simultaneous with the deafening explosion, Gunner Horace Bailey glimpsed a vivid flash through the porthole over his bunk. Before he had time to collect his scattered wits, the ship gave a violent lurch to port and he was catapulted out of the bunk. Still dazed, he scrambled to his feet and shot through the cabin doorway. No alarm bells had been sounded, but Bailey was in no doubt that the ship had been torpedoed.

The gunner fought his way out of the accommodation through an escape hatch, which was partially blocked by a jumble of planks and baulks of timber that had once supported the crates of aircraft on deck. As he threw aside the wreckage and tumbled out on the deck, the ship gave another violent lurch. Bailey was knocked off his feet and rolled across the deck towards the scuppers, crying out in pain as jagged metal cut into his bare feet and legs.

Holding back the rising panic, Bailey regained his feet and looked around him. He was alone on the after deck, surrounded by crumpled aircraft fuselages and smashed timbers. The ship's list was increasing alarmingly and she was down by the stern. The path to the boat deck, where Bailey hoped others were lowering the lifeboats, although he could hear no voices, was completely blocked by debris. Painfully, he clawed his way aft, planning to launch the liferaft stowed on the port side of the after masthouse. When he reached the masthouse he found the raft was no longer there, blown clean away by blast of the torpedo.

Sick with disappointment and racked by indecision, Bailey stood at the ship's side rail and gazed down into the sea, now only a few feet below the deck. It was then that he realized that in the fight to break clear of the accommodation he had left his lifejacket behind.

There was no turning back now. The list had become alarming and the sea below was coming nearer with every second that passed. Bailey climbed onto the rail and prepared to jump. At

132

that moment the *Fort Mumford* gave a last dying lurch and began to roll over. Bailey lost his grip and fell outwards.

Although the sea was pleasantly warm, to Bailey it had the chill of death about it as it closed over him and he sank deep. He was aware of pieces of wreckage swirling around him, brushing against his body. The ship was coming down on top of him and he was convinced that the time had come for Horace Bailey to die. He let his body go limp and was about to empty his lungs and finish it quickly when the instinct to survive took over.

When his lungs seemed on the point of bursting, Bailey suddenly found himself free of the wreckage and shooting upwards. He surfaced near a large floating object that looked similar in size and shape to a liferaft. Kicking out, he swam towards it and dragged himself aboard, discovering he was on a flat hull section of a landing craft which was once lashed down on the *Fort Mumford*'s deck. The craft would never see the beaches of Sicily where it had been destined to come ashore, but it might well save the life of Seaman Gunner Horace Bailey.

Having reached a place of refuge, Bailey's next move was to look around for other survivors. Standing erect, he searched the horizon all around, straining his eyes to pierce the hazy darkness. The *Fort Mumford* carried a total crew of fifty-three and, although she had gone down in a few minutes, it seemed inconceivable that Bailey could be the only survivor. And yet he could see no movement in the water, no bobbing red lifejacket lights and, more ominous, no voices. All around him there was darkness and silence, broken only by the slap of the waves on his waterlogged craft. His shoulders slumped and he sank back on his knees.

After ten minutes or so reflecting on the enormity of his predicament, Bailey thought he heard faint shouts and his spirits soared. Getting to his feet again, he cupped his hands and called out to the unknown voice. There was no reply. He continued calling until he was hoarse, pleading with the other men, if there were any, to answer. But there was only silence again. Then he saw what appeared to be a small fire floating on the water – possibly a lifejacket light – and he began calling again. Then the glow was gone as suddenly as it had appeared and the darkness

133

once more closed in around him and he was lonely and without hope. What Bailey had seen and heard can only be guessed at, but it seems possible that the voices were Japanese and the red glow the flash of *I-27*'s exhaust as she motored away from the scene of her night's work.

A black depression descended on Bailey and he felt his life had sunk to its lowest ebb. The sinking of his ship, his only home for more than three months, was a cruel enough blow. If others had survived with him, and he knew now that none had, he could have drawn comfort from their presence, and with it hope. But to suffer in this empty ocean alone, to drift for days, perhaps weeks, with only the oblivion of death to look forward to, was a prospect that filled him with dread.

While he was reviewing the hopelessness of his position, Bailey noticed he had blood on his hands. This puzzled him for a moment, then he felt the pain and he remembered his fall on deck when the dying *Fort Mumford* had given her second violent lurch. Feeling with tentative fingers, he discovered deep lacerations to his legs and feet, presumably caused by nails or jagged metal in the wreckage of the deck cargo. One cut in his foot went almost to the bone and was bleeding profusely.

A lesser man would have been tempted to lie down and wait for death, but Bailey, having come to terms with his plight, had ideas to the contrary. He cleaned his wounds with salt water and stopped the bleeding by plugging the deep cut in his foot with algae-like scum scooped up from the surface of the sea. From then on he knew his life depended on his own willpower and the mercy of God, who had deemed that he alone should survive the sinking of the *Fort Mumford*.

For the next five days he drifted, clinging to the waterlogged section of landing craft, his legs and back immersed in the sea for much of the time. He had no food or water, and no equipment other than a small canvas ammunition box cover and a short length of timber, both of which he had instinctively rescued from the sea as they drifted by. There was hardly a breath of wind and during the day the sun beat down on his half-naked body, burning his skin to a dark mahogany. Oddly enough, he felt no hunger, but he suffered agonies of thirst. Shoals of small fish swam around and nuzzled at the edges of his raft. He made desperate efforts to catch one of these, but for a long time they eluded him. Eventually, he caught a fish by the tail and snatched it out of the water. But by this time he was so weak he was unable to kill the poor struggling creature and returned it to the sea.

At times, he became feverish, hallucinating, but it was his injured leg that caused him most concern; it appeared to be growing thinner, almost withering before his eyes. It was perhaps this preoccupation with the state of his leg that kept him sane in the end. The turning point came on the fourth day when an isolated shower of rain swept across the raft and Bailey was able at last to quench his thirst, licking the rain drops as they ran down his body. His spirits began to rise again.

On the fifth day he saw a white bird swooping low over the sea in the distance. For several minutes he watched, envying the bird's ability to skim over the waves. Then, as it rose above the horizon, the white bird became a sail, and below the sail the hull of a small craft came in sight. Trembling with excitement, Bailey snatched up the pieces of flotsam he had so providentially collected. Working quickly, he tied the scrap of canvas to the broken plank, producing a makeshift signal flag, which he waved frantically above his head. Before long he found himself being handed gently over the bulwarks of the small boat.

When his thirst had been slaked by a cup of water, Bailey was given a concoction of Eucalyptus oil and water, which appeared to act as a stimulant to his tired brain. His rescuers informed him that he was on board an Indian dhow bound from the Malabar Coast to Mikindani in Tanganyika. The dhow was of about 47 tons displacement and carried a crew of nine, who treated Bailey with extreme kindness. On seeing the state of his injured leg, which had turned quite black, the sturdy brown men held him down while they scrubbed the leg with boiling water. The agony Bailey went through was intense, but there is no doubt that the rough and ready Indian antisepsis saved his leg, which thereafter began to heal cleanly.

Running before the prevailing north-easterly wind, which was light but steady, the dhow reached Mikindani on 7 May, forty-three days after Bailey had been picked up. The seaman gunner walked ashore in Tanganyika with only a slight limp to betray the ordeal he had survived. As to the men who saved his life, the only clue he had to their identity was the number of their dhow, 443.

The mystery of the disappearance of Captain John Reardon Smith and the other fifty-one men of the *Fort Mumford* will probably never be solved. The ship was torpedoed at 8 o'clock in the night, when the watches were changing and, consequently, very few crew members would have yet been in their bunks. Although she sank quite quickly, it seems, as evidenced by Horace Bailey's actions before he was pitched overboard, there should have been ample time for many more men to get clear before the ship went down. The Japanese were notorious for killing survivors after sinking a ship, so it could be that the voices Bailey heard were those of his shipmates pleading for mercy. On the other hand it may be that others survived and, like Bailey, drifted on bits of wreckage for days, before dying of thirst and exposure. Some wreckage, identified as coming from the *Fort Mumford*, was washed up on Cape Comorin, 500 miles to the east of the sinking, but no bodies were ever found.

After sinking the *Fort Mumford*, Toshiaki Fukumura went from strength to strength, sinking in the nine months that followed eight Allied ship totalling nearly 43,000 tons. His last act of war was to sink the British troopship *Khedive Ismail* near Addu Atoll on 12 February 1944. The British ship, which went down in two minutes, was carrying 1,847 passengers and crew, including British, American and African troops, and members of the Women's Services. More than 1000 lives were lost. However, retribution was swift, *I-27* being sunk with all hands by the British destroyers *Petard* and *Paladin*, which were escorting the troopship.

19

Operation 'Husky'

It might truly be said that the eighteen months spent in the Mediterranean by *U-375* up until June 1943 had not been an unqualified success. Under her commander, Kapitänleutnant Jürgen Könenkamp, she had covered many thousands of miles and succeeded in sinking only two small ships, the 190-ton British armed trawler *Vassiliki* and a Palestinian coaster of 558 tons. She had also damaged the minelayer HMS *Manxman*, which Könenkamp erroneously claimed to be a London-class cruiser, and the British merchantman *Empire Kumasi* of 6288 tons. The *Empire Kumasi* was towed into Haifa and subsequently declared a total loss, but she could only legitimately be marked on *U-375*'s score sheet as 'damaged'. By July 1943 Könenkamp's prospects of amassing sufficient tonnage sunk to justify his continued presence in the Mediterranean seemed very poor indeed. However, an opportunity of increasing his score, the like of which had never been seen before in the Mediterranean, was about to come his way.

Some two weeks before Könenkamp had logged his first meagre sinking, the Casablanca Conference had agreed that the first large-scale entry of Allied forces into Europe would be made through the island of Sicily. By the time German and Italian forces in Tunisia surrendered on 12 May the invasion plans had been finalized and the date set for 9 July. Although it was known that Sicily was inadequately defended, the planners had no wish to repeat the 1942 Dieppe fiasco, which itself was a trial run for the invasion of Europe. Accordingly, the Sicily landings were planned on a massive and, hopefully, unstoppable scale. In

Operation 'Husky', as the invasion was codenamed, a total 2,700 ships carrying troops, armour and supplies were to be involved. In all, thirty-four separate convoys would set out from the United Kingdom, Malta and the Eastern Mediterranean, converging on the Sicilian beaches on the night of 9/10 July and on the days immediately following. The tideless sea would soon be covered in ships from horizon to horizon.

The *St Essylt*, a 1941-built motorship of 5634 tons, owned by the South American Saint Line, had neither been designed nor constructed as a troopship. Nevertheless, in June 1943 she found herself in Glasgow taking on board, in addition to 900 tons of military stores, over 300 men of the Canadian First Division. With her crew increased to seventy-nine by the addition of an extra twelve DEMS gunners, the *St Essylt* left the Clyde for the beaches of Sicily with a total of 401 personnel on board. In her holds she carried military vehicles stowed on top of cases of ammunition and stores, while the two landing craft that would put the Canadians ashore were lashed on top of her No.2 hatch. Her defensive armament consisted of the usual stern-mounted 4-inch, a 40mm Bofors anti-aircraft gun, eight Oerlikons, two twin Marlin machine guns and various anti-aircraft rockets.

At the Tail of the Bank the *St Essylt*, commanded by Captain S. Diggins, formed up with the seventeen other similarly loaded ships of Convoy KMS 18B and sailed from the Clyde on 24 June. The *St Essylt*, unusually for a cargo carrier of her day, was capable of a sustained speed of 15 knots, and Captain Diggins was far from pleased to find himself sailing as rear ship of the outer port column in a convoy which was to saunter along at a mere 8 knots. With the German U-boats capable of 17 knots on the surface and 7½ knots submerged, this seemed to be tempting providence. And the *St Essylt*, as tail-end Charlie of KMS 18B, would be one of the first in the line of fire.

But, at least so far as the Atlantic passage of the voyage was concerned, Diggins had little to fear from the U-boats. The increased use of radar-equipped aircraft by the Allies had resulted in the loss of forty-one U-boats in the first three weeks of May and more and more pressure was being put on the enemy. It was rumoured – and the rumour was true – that Dönitz had withdrawn the majority of his wolf packs from the North Atlantic. It was not surprising then, that the convoy's eight-day passage from the Clyde to Gibraltar, via the north of Ireland, passed without incident. No U-boat warnings were received from the Admiralty and no hostile craft sighted or detected. The absence of the enemy was almost uncanny.

The second day of July saw KMS 18B steaming through the Straits of Gibraltar with the land in sight on both sides. The convoy then had just over 1000 miles to cover to its appointment with the island of Sicily, which was already being softened up by saturation bombing by Allied aircraft. On 4 July, when American troops assembling for embarkation in the North African ports were enjoying a subdued celebration of their Independence Day, KMS 18B was closing the coast of Algeria, some 600 miles from its destination. All ships in the convoy were keeping Double British Summertime (GMT +2), so that by the time the sun was setting astern that night convoy time was 2100. In the advancing twilight the rocky promontory of Cape Tenez was just visible to the south-east at 25 miles.

The troops crowding the decks of the *St Essylt* looked longingly at the distant land, for the Mediterranean was not living up to their expectations. A fresh easterly wind had whipped up a short, rough sea, which gave the ship an uncomfortable corkscrewing motion. For Jürgen Könenkamp the agitation of the sea was a welcome asset, hiding the wake of his periscope as he brought *U-375* into a favourable position to start his attack on the convoy. His first torpedo hit the 8762-ton British cargo vessel *City of Venice*, lead ship of Column 2.

Captain Diggins was on the bridge of the *St Essylt* when the *City of Venice*, close on the starboard side, sent her distress rockets skywards. He took immediate steps to bring his own ship into a state of readiness. Action Stations was sounded on the alarm bells, all troops were ordered out of the messdecks, extra lookouts posted and all guns manned. At the same time the Convoy Commodore, for some reason beyond explanation, ordered all ships to cease zig-zagging and reduce speed to 7 knots. The effect of this action was to give Könenkamp a huge and unexpected advantage. He made full use of it.

At 2145 the *St Essylt*, maintaining a steady course of 080° and as ordered, making revolutions for 7 knots, was hit by a torpedo in the starboard side of her No. 2 hold. The force of the explosion erupted through the hatchtop, smashing and overturning the big landing craft stowed athwartships on the hatch. Flames and smoke poured out of the hold, indicating that the vehicles stowed below had caught fire. The ship took a heavy list to starboard as the sea poured into her. Diggins, showing commendable calm under the circumstances, stopped his engines and ordered his wireless operator to transmit a message informing the rest of the convoy of the *St Essylt*'s plight.

The fire in the forward hold quickly became an inferno, flames shooting over 100 feet into the air. These set alight the ammunition and petrol stowed on the deck and the whole of the fore deck became enveloped in flame and smoke. Diggins accepted that there was little hope for the ship and he must now think about saving the men in his charge.

To accommodate her enlarged complement of 401 in an emergency, the *St Essylt* carried, in addition to her four lifeboats, numerous liferafts and small floats. Even with a rough sea running, Diggins did not anticipate much diffculty in launching these, but it was obvious that, with so many men to get clear, the evacuation of the ship would take some time. And in order to avoid unnecessary loss of life this evacuation must be carried out with the minimum of panic.

The order to abandon ship was quietly passed by word of mouth and, supervised by the *St Essylt*'s crew, the Canadian troops began to leave the burning ship. Despite the heavy list, exploding ammunition and flaming drums of petrol adding to the horrors of the night, the evacuation took place calmly and relatively unhurried. Due largely to the tight discipline of the troops and the unruffled efficiency of their officers, all were off the ship in less than half an hour after she had been hit.

The operation was not to go completely smoothly, however. The *St Essylt*'s four lifeboats were soon full and the majority of the survivors were forced to jump into the sea to take their chances with the rafts and floats. Those unfortunate enough to

140

find themselves clinging to the floats suffered harsh treatment at the hands of the rough seas, resulting in many of them clambering aboard the already overcrowded lifeboats, sinking them to the gunwales. Panic broke out when those in the boats realized the danger, but, again through the tight discipline of the Canadian troops, order was soon restored and men redistributed on to liferafts while the boats were bailed out.

While all this was happening Captain Diggins had remained on the bridge of his ship. With him were a small band of volunteers who had stayed behind to clear away the boats and rafts and, if possible, to save the ship. They were Chief Officer D. Robertson, Second Engineer R. Tucker, Sergeant G. W. Brown and Lance Bombardier G.A. Bassett, two of the DEMS gunners, and Sergeant R. Hillcoat and Bombardier R.N. Ritchie of the Royal Candian Army.

When all the boats and rafts were away Diggins led his party forward to take a closer look at the fire. Unfortunately, a fresh series of explosions broke out as they made their way up the fore deck and flying debris and exploding tracers forced them to retire to the safety of the after deck. If the means had been available, Diggins would have then abandoned the ship altogether, but not even a small float remained to support them in the water. He decided that staying aboard to await rescue might be the lesser of two evils.

At about 2230 the corvette HMS *Honeysuckle* arrived, and began picking up men from the water around the *St Essylt*. In spite of the heavy seas running, *Honeysuckle*'s boats did magnificent work, snatching the exhausted soldiers from the rafts and ferrying them to the corvette. *Honeysuckle* was soon joined by a second corvette, HMS *Rhododendron*, and a naval salvage tug, HMS *Restive*.

While the rescue continued Captain Diggins and his party were crouched in the shelter of the *St Essylt*'s poop deckhouse. The explosions on the burning fore deck were by then merging into one continuous roll of thunder and the flames were steadily advancing aft. Reluctantly, Diggins was now forced to accept that they must leave the ship soon or be burnt alive as she went down. He therefore ordered Chief Officer Robertson to signal

Honeysuckle with his torch. When the corvette, which was still scooping men up from the water, offered to close the ship to take them off, Diggins insisted that she finish her rescue work first.

A few moments later the situation aboard the *St Essylt* became critical when a stack of boxed ammunition on the fore deck exploded with a tremendous roar. Smoke and flames billowed aft, threatening to engulf the seven men crouching in the shelter of the deckhouse. If they were to save their lives they must go now. Diggins instructed Robertson to contact *Honeysuckle* again to warn her that they were abandoning ship. The corvette immediately moved in, but the smoke and flame, the flying debris and exploding ammunition prevented her from coming alongside. There was no alternative but to take to the water and, handing his lifejacket to one of the Canadians who was unable to swim, Diggins led the way over the side.

In his battle with the sea, turned blood red by the flames from his burning ship, Diggins lost touch with the others, but he was a strong swimmer and was soon pulling himself up the corvette's scrambling net. Once aboard *Honeysuckle*, he made straight for the bridge to advise on the possible location of the men still in the water. When the others who had stood by with him to the last on the *St Essylt* had been picked up, Diggins, although by now in a state of exhaustion, remained on the corvette's bridge assisting with the rescue operation.

By 0200 on the 5th, *Honeysuckle* had taken 276 men alive from the sea and, with *Rhododendron* and *Restive*, continued the search throughout the night. At 0545, when the rescue work was nearing its end, Diggins finally went below. Even as he lay down to rest the *St Essylt* blew up and by the time he reached the upper deck again she had gone.

The naval ships broke off the search at 0800 and set course for Algiers. In all, they had picked up 397 survivors from the *St Essylt*. The body of one of her stewards was found, but thirty-two Canadian servicemen were still missing. In view of the weather, the number of men involved and the volatile nature of the *St Essylt*'s cargo, her casualties were remarkably few. Much of the credit for this minor miracle must go to Captain Diggins, without whose cool overall direction of the abandonment, and his subsequent involvement in the search for survivors, many more men might have died.

There were other quiet heroes in evidence on that night and Diggins did not hesitate to name them in his report:-

Chief Officer D. Robertson: 'This officer was outstanding in his efforts in getting the crew and troops clear of the burning ship. He unhesitatingly volunteered to remain on board with me in case anything could be done to save the ship, and was remarkably cool and efficient throughout.'

Chief Engineer W. Marrs: 'Although the fore part of the ship was burning furiously, Mr Marrs went down into the engineroom to ascertain that all his staff were clear and also to stop pumps which were causing discharge likely to flood the lifeboats. He also did good work in maintaining discipline amongst the men in No.3 lifeboat when that boat became waterlogged and he assisted in towing several of the rafts clear of the burning vessel.'

Second Engineer R. Tucker: 'This officer volunteered to remain on board as long as he was required; he was the last but one to leave the vessel and throughout this trying ordeal was remarkably cool and calm.'

Able Seaman M McNeil: 'I consider that Able Seaman McNeil is a very fine sailor. When the forward fall of No.3 lifeboat went with a run, he stopped it by means of a rope stopper. The forward fall was again accidentally cut instead of the rope stopper, but with great presence of mind McNeil ran aft and cut the after fall, thereby allowing the boat to go down more or less on an even keel.'

Sgt. G.W. Brown and L/Bdr. G.A. Bassett, RA Maritime Regt: 'Both these men greatly assisted in getting men off the ship, after-wards volunteering to remain on board with the Chief Officer and myself in case their services were required.'

Major Ware, P.P.C.L.I, OC Troops: 'Major Ware was very calm and efficient throughout, assisting in getting his men orga-nized and away from the ship quickly and efficiently. When all his men were clear, he reported to me and asked if he could be of further assistance, but I ordered him to follow his men so he jumped overboard and swam to a raft.'

Lt. Merryweather RNVR (S.N.O.T): 'Lieutenant Merryweather was very calm and efficient and assisted in getting the men clear of the ship. He remained on board until ordered to abandon ship along with the OC Troops.'

Company Sgt. Major C.H. Blower: (1021 Docks Operating Company RE): 'Company Sgt. Major Blower did excellent work in assisting to get the troops into No.3 lifeboat. He remained on board to assist in releasing the rafts long after his own boat had pulled away from the ship.'

Sgt. R. Hillcoat and Bdr. R.N. Ritchie R.C.A: 'These men greatly assisted in getting the troops clear of the ship and voluntarily remained on board with me in case their assistance was required.'

The landings on Sicily were a complete success, only four ships being lost out of the 2,700 involved in the operation. The fighting on the island lasted for thirty-nine days, an armistice being signed on 3 September. On that same day the Allies crossed the Straits of Messina to the mainland of Italy.

U-375's uninspiring record in the Mediterranean ended with the sinking of the *St Essylt*. Twenty-six days later, on 30 July, she was cornered and sunk off Pantelleria by the US patrol vessel PC-624. Jürgen Könenkamp went down with his boat.

20

The U-Cruisers

The Indian Ocean, first revealed to European eyes when Batholomew Diaz rounded the Cape of Good Hope in 1488, may be likened to a great oceanic bay bounded by the continents of Africa, Asia and Australasia. It covers an area of some 17 million square miles and plunges to nearly 23,000 feet at its deepest point. This vast sweep of blue water is troubled seasonally by the stormy south-west monsoon and sporadically by the rampaging cyclone but being dominated for the most part by a permanent high pressure system, its weather is, in the main, benign.

At sunrise on 29 July 1943 the Indian Ocean eastwards of Madagascar was in one of its more playful moods. A brisk north-north-easterly breeze frothed the tops of a moderate swell, but the weather was fine and clear, with eye-stretching visibility. A lone ship, the *Cornish City*, dipped her bows easily into the swell as she steamed steadily north, making a shade under 10 knots. She was 240 miles off the coast of Madagascar and some 300 miles south of the island of Réunion, which she expected to pass at around noon on the following day.

On the *Cornish City*'s bridge Chief Officer K.E. Germaney, having finished his morning sights, was enjoying the sunrise and reflecting on the quirk of fate that had brought about his sudden promotion from second officer to chief officer less than two weeks earlier. His predecessor, injured in a shipboard accident, had been put into hospital at Lourenço Marques in Mozambique. As a result, overnight, Germaney found himself sewing on a third gold band and charged with, in addition to the

4 to 8 watch, the responsibility for the whole of the deck operations of the *Cornish City*. After the comparatively untaxing life he had enjoyed as ship's navigator and keeper of the middle watch, the challenge posed by his changed situation was somewhat daunting.

Captain Henry Issac chose that moment to join Germaney on the bridge. To Issac the sun rising over an empty and apparently friendly sea was yet another blessing to be counted. Having survived nearly four years of this bitter conflict at sea, Issac was only too aware that he might be living on borrowed time. But hope, like the sun on that clear, fine morning, was rising steadily. He had seen British shipping losses peak at nearly 500,000 tons a month in the winter of 1942, then fall off dramatically as the escorts gained superiority over the U-boats. Crossing the North Atlantic was still no Sunday afternoon jaunt across the Channel – even in time of peace it never would be – but for the merchant seaman the odds in favour of survival had shortened considerably. Now, with Italy on the verge of surrender, the Germans running out of steam in Russia and the Americans beginning to flush the Japanese out of the Pacific islands, it seemed possible that this war would soon be over. Issac considered that both he and the *Cornish City* might, after all, live to see a return to the days when men could again sail the seas without fear of death and destruction. Meanwhile, this Indian Ocean passage, with its unlikelihood of molestation by the enemy, was a bonus to be savoured.

Issac's confidence in the benignity of the Indian Ocean was only partly justified. After the disappearance of the surface raiders from the scene, the striking power of the Axis in these waters was limited to a handful of German and Japanese submarines. Five of these boats, *U-172*, *U-177*, *U-178*, *U-181* and *U-182*, Dönitz's long-range U-cruisers, first rounded the Cape in October 1942. In the intervening months they had wreaked considerable havoc among merchant shipping in the Indian Ocean, but they were all now reaching the end of their endurance. At the beginning of May 1943 nine other U-boats had set out from Biscay ports with the intention of relieving the long-serving five, but they had been so dogged by bad luck and harassed by Allied aircraft that they were unlikely to arrive in the Indian Ocean before September, if at all. Informed of this situation, those U-boats awaiting relief had once again filled their bunker tanks from the supply ship *Charlotte Schliemann* at a secret rendezvous south of Madagascar and then gone their separate ways in search of new victims.

The *Cornish City* was not as long away from home as the U-boats, having left Britain in mid-February with a cargo for South African ports. She was a 4895-ton motorship, built in 1936, and carried a crew of forty-three, including four young apprentices and six DEMS gunners. She was armed with a 4-inch and 12-pounder aft, four twin-barrelled machine guns on her bridge and six rocket launchers, sufficient for her to put up a credible resistance when attacked from the air or by a vessel on the surface. As was the case with most Allied merchant ships, she had no defence against a submerged submarine.

The long sojourn discharging cargo in the South African ports, which overflowed with the good things of life and offered lavish, open-hearted hospitality, had been sheer delight for Henry Issac and his men. When the ship finally left Durban on the morning of 22 July, loaded with 9,600 tons of coal for Aden, they were ready to return to the realities of war with good heart. Riding the long Southern Ocean rollers stiffly as she cleared the break-waters of Durban harbour, the *Cornish City* joined up with Convoy DN 53.

Compared with the huge 40-ship convoys of the North Atlantic, with their attendant destroyers, corvettes and occasional aircraft carrier, DN 53 was something of an anti-climax. This mini-convoy consisted of only five merchant ships, escorted by two enthusiastic but painfully ineffectual armed trawlers of the South African Navy. The only comfort Captain Issac was able to draw from the presence of the trawlers was that they were at least equipped with Asdic and would be able to give warning of the presence of a submerged U-boat. Beyond that, there seemed to be little point to the ships keeping company. The main object of the convoy was to see the heavily-loaded merchantmen past the southern entrance to the Mozambique Channel, a hunting ground of long standing for German and Japanese

147

U-boats. This was achieved by sunset on the 24th and the convoy was then dispersed. It was with no misgivings that Issac set course for the Gulf of Aden and rang for full speed. From then on he alone would control the destiny of his ship and his men. He was not to know that this control would shortly pass from his hands.

Korvettenkapitän Robert Gysae had, like Henry Issac, experienced all the horrors of the Battle of the Atlantic, albeit from the other side of the periscope. In *U-98* he had sunk ten ships, totalling 52,025 tons, over the period from March 1941 to February 1942, all the while enduring the rigours of the angry seas and suffering the frenzied onslaughts of the defending escorts. In October 1942 Gysae, in command of *U-177*, had entered the Indian Ocean in company with the other U-cruisers. Working his way across the Cape shipping lanes to the Mozambique Channel, the seasoned hunter had increased his personal score by nearly 72,000 tons. At the end of June, having taken fuel, fresh torpedoes and supplies from the *Charlotte Schliemann*, he decided to cast his net to the east of Madagascar.

29 July was just another routine day in the life of the *Cornish City*, normal shipboard life proceeding as it had from the day she left the shipyard. War or no war, there were decks to be scrubbed, cargo gear to overhaul, creeping rust to be attended to. At 0935, with breakfast out of the way, Captain Issac and Chief Officer Germaney walked the port wing of the lower bridge, discussing priorities and programmes. With the warm sun shining down out of a blue sky dotted with fair-weather cumulus and the horizon empty as far as the eye could see, it was a good day for making plans. Neither man saw the track of *U-177*'s torpedo as it raced in on the port side.

Gysae's aim was precise and achieved the desired result. His torpedo struck the unsuspecting ship in the vicinity of the water-tight bulkhead between her engine-room and No.4 hold. Deafened by the explosion, Chief Officer Germaney watched in horror as the port side of the boat deck erupted in a great sheet of flame which reached over 100 feet into the air, taking the shattered remains of the port side lifeboat with it.

With her engine-room and adjacent hold flooding, the

148

Cornish City began to sink at once, going down by the stern. Realizing he had to act quickly, Germaney ran to the starboard side of the boat deck, where he found some of the crew had already lowered the lifeboat to the water. It lay alongside, rising and falling on the swell. He glanced aft, to where the sea was now washing over the deck, and as he did the *Cornish City* seemed to give a violent shudder. Captain Issac, who was leaning out over the rail of the lower bridge, shouted a warning. Moments later Germaney saw the bows rear up in the air, while the deck he was standing on remained level. The *Cornish City* had broken her back.

Keeping a tight rein on his rising panic, Germaney slipped his lifejacket over his head and just had time to tie one of the tapes when the ship began to sink beneath him. As he went under he saw the starboard lifeboat, still made fast to the ship, dragged back on board and into the maelstrom she created as she went down. There were six men in the boat, their faces white, their mouths gaping wide open as the awfulness of their predicament dawned on them.

Buoyed up by his lifejacket, Germaney shot to the surface, only to find when he looked around that both his ship and the lifeboat had gone. The torpedoing and subsequent sinking of the *Cornish City* had taken no more than two minutes.

After about half an hour in the water with his mind running the gamut of fear, panic and despair, Germaney could hardly believe his luck when a liferaft drifted past. He was hauled on board by the two occupants, the *Cornish City*'s Estonian-born boatswain Grant and Fifth Engineer Plewes. The raft was one of the new DAB-type, supplied before the ship left the United Kingdom. It was a substantial wooden craft of about ten feet by six feet, with a shaped bow and stern, and a drop-keel.

As he lay gasping on the raft Germaney saw the submarine surfacing only yards away. His immediate reaction was to slip off his lifejacket and struggle out of his sodden uniform jacket with its tell-tale gold bands. He would rather take his chance with the sea than become a prisoner of the men who had sunk his ship.

The submarine, effectively camouflaged with alternate light

and dark grey stripes, and armed with what looked like a 3-inch gun on deck and an anti-aircraft cannon in her conning tower, cautiously closed the raft. She carried no visible identification marks and flew no ensign, but the six men in her conning tower, two officers with high-crowned caps and four ratings scanning the horizon with binoculars, were obviously German.

When the raft bumped alongside the casing of the U-boat, one of the officers, a big man with dark hair and a beard, whom Germaney took to be the commander, leaned over the conning tower and addressed the survivors in English. Gysae's questions were predictable and to the point. He demanded to know the name of the ship he had sunk, her port of registry, last port of call, her destination and her cargo.

The sea around them being covered in a film of coal dust, the nature of the *Cornish City*'s cargo was obvious, but Germaney refused to divulge any more than her name. Gysae persisted with his questioning, but Germaney stubbornly refused to answer which, considering the vulnerable position of the survivors, was a brave if futile gesture. But Gysae was patient. He continued the one-sided interrogation for a while and then gave up in disgust. Germaney then had the audacity to ask for some cigarettes and, not surprisingly, Gysae refused. He did, however, wish the survivors good luck and promised to send a wireless message to all ships reporting their position. With a quick wave, he then backed the U-boat away from the raft and made off on the surface, heading in a north-westerly direction.

While he was being questioned, Germaney became aware of another smaller liferaft, with three men aboard, drifting about 200 yards away and, as soon as the U-boat was out of sight, he brought the two rafts together. The three men on the small raft were Apprentice E. Hall, Ordinary Seaman Millard and DEMS gunner Able Seaman W.E. Fletcher. Together with Germaney, Grant and Pewes, they were all that remained of the *Cornish City*'s crew of forty-three.

Germaney took command of the little band of survivors, transferring the newcomers to his own raft, which was better equipped and had ample room for six men. The provisions and water were taken from the small raft, which was then set adrift.

Later in the day another DAB raft was found, probably having come to the surface after the ship went down. The two rafts were lashed together and, after taking an inventory of both, Germaney estimated that, with care, they had sufficient water, Horlicks tablets, chocolate and biscuits to last them for 100 days. The rafts also had sails, canvas spray screens, sea anchors and smoke floats. Given all this, their hopes of survival were excellent, providing they were not unfortunate enough to be caught by a cyclone. Madagascar, the nearest land, lay 250 or so miles to the west, but before attempting to set sail Germaney decided it would be prudent to remain in the vicinity of the sinking for twenty-four hours in case a search was being made for them.

During the rest of that day the two tethered rafts drifted with their sea anchors streamed. To while away the time, the survivors exchanged experiences. Following the torpedoing of the ship, their individual escapes had been narrow ones, but none more so than that of Fifth Engineer Plewes. The explosion had trapped him in his cabin and he was forced to attempt to escape through a porthole overlooking an outboard alleyway. The opening was a fraction too small for his hips and he ended up jammed in the porthole, able to move neither in nor out. Fortunately for Plewes, help arrived in the form of Assistant Engineer Norman Bradley, who ran through the alleyway, heading for the after deck. Bradley stopped, helped to prise Plewes from the porthole and the two men then went over the side together. Norman Bradley was never seen again.

Seaman Gunner Fletcher, without thought for his own safety, rushed aft to the 4-inch when the torpedo struck. Although he was alone and the gun deck by then awash, Fletcher loaded the gun and trained it on the conning tower of the U-boat. However, before he was able to fire, the ship sank under him and he was washed into the sea. It was Fletcher's opinion that, had he been given another thirty seconds at the gun, *U-177* might well have joined the *Cornish City* on the bottom.

The night of the 29th was long, but the survivors were reasonably comfortable and in good heart. Next morning they breakfasted well on their emergency rations and settled down to

151

discuss the possibility of sailing to Madagascar. At 1130 they were about to make sail when they sighted an aircraft low down on the southern horizon. As the plane drew nearer, on what appeared to be a deliberate search pattern, it became recognizable as a Catalina flying boat.

Germaney attempted to set off a smoke float, but this stubbornly refused to light. The others, fearful that the plane might pass by without seeing them, tore down the orange canvas spray screens and waved them frantically over their heads. Unlike the smoke float, their makeshift distress signals worked. The Catalina, then about 5 miles off, suddenly banked and flew directly over the rafts.

For the next three and a half hours the Catalina circled the rafts. A package was dropped, but landed too far away for the survivors to reach it, but later the plane followed up with a tin of cigarettes tied to an inflated Mae West. This was recovered and the delighted survivors found a note inside the tin informing them that the Navy was on the way.

At about 1500, the Catalina gave one final dip of its wings and flew off. Once again alone on an empty ocean, an air of hopelessness settled over the drifting rafts. To counteract this Germaney organized the men into watches. He saved the most punishing middle watch for himself and at midnight sat with his back to the mast to wait out the darkest hours of the night. At about 0320 on the 31st, when Germaney's spirits were at their lowest ebb and his eyelids drooping, he saw a flashing light reflecting on the clouds.

It could have been just lightning, but the flashes continued and to a regular pattern. Germaney forced himself awake and it slowly dawned on him that the light was flashing the morse letters VE, a code signal used by the Royal Navy for calling up merchant ships. He woke the others, but was wary of answering the signal in case the U-boat might still be in the vicinity. But the flashing persisted, with the unseen lamp searching around the horizon, and Germaney at last set off a distress flare. Shortly before 0500, with the dawn still an hour away, the British destroyer *Denizen* found the rafts, and the survivors were taken on board. They were landed at Port Louis, Mauritius, on 1

August, very little worse for their experience. On going ashore Germaney was informed that their prompt rescue was due to a brief wireless transmission giving their position picked up by Colombo Radio. The source of the message was unknown, but as no distress had been sent out by the *Cornish City*'s operator, there was no doubt in Germaney's mind that Robert Gysae had kept his promise to them.

Nothing was ever heard of the thirty-six men missing with the *Cornish City* and it must be assumed that they went down with the ship. *U-177*, last seen by Germaney heading to the west-north-west on the 29th, sank the 4195-ton Greek steamer *Efthalia Mari* five days later. And that was to be her last conquest. In February 1944, when unsuccessfully trawling the South Atlantic for victims, she was sunk by an American Liberator on patrol from Ascension Island. Robert Gysae survived the sinking and the rest of the war, later to become a Fleet-Admiral in Germany's new peacetime navy.

21

The Old Ones Die Hard

By the late summer of 1943 the North Atlantic was rapidly returning to its normal role of being no more than an ocean perpetually troubled by the in-fighting of the warm and cold air masses that clash over its deep waters. After the massacre of the U-boats in May of that year, when more than forty failed to return to their bases, it appeared that Admiral Dönitz had at last accepted defeat in the West. In August only six U-boats remained at large in the Atlantic, sinking in that month just four Allied merchantmen.

In September, however, Dönitz decided to make one more bid to cut Britain's Atlantic arteries, through which were flowing vast quantities of arms and equipment for the forthcoming invasion of France. A force of twenty-eight U-boats, including the 'milch cow' *U-460*, was despatched westwards from the Biscay bases. One of their number was *U-161*, commanded by Kapitänleutnant Albrecht Achilles. On his previous Atlantic patrol, in the spring of 1943, Achilles had suffered the gross humiliation of sinking only one ship – and that the Canadian sailing vessel *Angelus* of only 255 tons. Achilles, determined to avoid a repeat of this fiasco, headed for the coast of Brazil after clearing Biscay, working on the assumption that potential targets in that area did not enjoy the massive sea and air protection afforded those in the North Atlantic.

Some three months earlier South American Saint Line's *St Usk* had loaded at London and slipped down Channel bound for her peacetime trading grounds, the east coast of South America. To say that the 5472-ton *St Usk* was 'long in the tooth' would be an understatement. She had, in fact, been built in 1909, at a time when the last great windjammers were still beating their way around Cape Horn. Having survived the Great War and twenty-one years of the gruelling charter market, the *St Usk* was in the summer of 1943 well past pensionable age and in the fourth year of her second world war. Commanded by Captain G.H. Moss, she was a tall-masted, five-hatch, single-screw steamer, still capable, for all her great age, of a sea speed of 9 knots. She was manned by a crew of forty-eight, including six DEMS gunners, and mounted a 12-pounder forward, a 4-inch aft and four 20mm Oerlikons and two twin Marlins about her bridge and funnel deck. On her incident-free outward voyage, in convoy to Freetown, and then unescorted across the South Atlantic, these guns had lain idle, except for the occasional practice shoot.

Begun in a London made grey and lifeless by the privations of a long war, every day of the 28-day passage had been seen by Captain Moss and his crew as a step further into the beckoning sunrise. Throughout the weather held fine, the sea was in a gentle mood and the enemy was conspicuous by his absence. Then, at the end of the long run there was Brazil, a lush, green land with frightening extremes of poverty and wealth, but so far removed from the war as to be on another planet. Discharging the outward cargo and loading produce for home had been a long, unhurried business, but two months' indulgence in this unreal paradise had proved quite enough for the men of the *St Usk*. When the time came to close the hatches and head northwards again, they were ready to return to the other world.

The harbour of Rio de Janeiro is said to be the most beautiful in the world; surrounded by massive forest-clad mountains, it is certainly one of the most impressive. It is also the largest natural deep-water harbour in the world, capable of sheltering a vast number of ocean-going ships at any one time. At five o'clock on the afternoon of 15 September 1943, with only an hour or so of daylight left, the *St Usk* sailed from this great harbour, loaded with 6,500 tons of cargo. She was to proceed independently to Freetown and there join a convoy for the United Kingdom, back-tracking exactly on her outward passage in the early summer.

The *St Usk*'s course to Sierra Leone lay directly across the old sailing ship routes to and from the Horn, passing midway between St Paul Rocks and Ascension Island. At her estimated speed of 9 knots, the passage was expected to take eighteen days, with the south-east trades blowing abaft her starboard beam and urging her on for much of the way. According to information received by Captain Moss prior to sailing, there were no U-boats known to be operating in the area his ship would pass through.

Moss's intelligence proved to be in error. Forty-eight hours out of Rio de Janeiro, on the 17th, a warning was received from the Admiralty of the presence of a U-boat detected in the *St Usk*'s path and a diversion was recommended and made. Captain Moss also took the precaution of posting extra lookouts. Two more days passed peacefully, but, at 1710 on the afternoon of the 19th, a heavy shock was felt by those in the after part of the ship. Below decks, in the engine-room, the bump was sufficient to throw the lubricating oil out of the oil well of the propeller shaft thrust block, indicating to the engineer of the watch that they must have struck a sizeable object.

On the bridge, some 40 feet above the waterline, Chief Officer E.C. Martyn had felt nothing unusual. Had he done so, he might well have concluded that the ship had collided with a whale, a not uncommon happening in these waters. However, Martyn's equanimity was soon disturbed by the jangling of the after telephone bell. Picking up the receiver, he heard the breathless voice of the DEMS gunner on watch at the 4-inch reporting the bump and adding that a periscope was visible 20 yards off the port quarter and overtaking the ship. Recovering from the shock of the news, Martyn ordered the helm hard to starboard to sheer the ship away from the danger and then called the Captain to the bridge.

The periscope was no longer visible when Moss arrived on the bridge moments later. On being briefed on the situation, he put the ship on a zig-zag pattern and called for the carpenter to sound round to see if the hull was breached. The results of the soundings proved negative, leaving Moss with a puzzle on his hands. The shock clearly felt on the after deck and in the engine-room had not been imagined, but could conceivably be put down to a basking whale, or even a sunken ship floating just below the surface – there were many such submerged wrecks drifting in the ocean in these violent days of war. The matter of the periscope – and the gunner was adamant that he had seen one – was more worrying. Could it be that a U-boat had been shadowing them and had inadvertently collided with the ship? Nothing more was seen and as soon as darkness fell Moss discontinued the zig-zag and made all possible speed on a steady course.

At twenty minutes before midnight Moss was again called to the bridge, Third Officer R.H. Russel reporting having felt two heavy bumps forward with an interval of two or three minutes between them. He described them as 'muffled thuds' and this description was confirmed by some crew members whose accommodation was right forward, under the forecastle head. The lookouts had seen nothing.

There was now no doubt in Moss's mind that they were being shadowed by a submarine – and a pretty clumsy one at that. But he still could not be sure and was reluctant to start a furore by transmitting the SSSS (I am under attack by submarine) message. Not that there would have been much response. Allied naval ships were very thin on the water in this area and any plea for help was unlikely to be answered. Moss decided to keep radio silence and hope for the best.

Chief Officer Martyn heard the news of the latest incident when he took up the watch at 0400 on the 20th. The *St Usk* had by then moved a further 40 miles to the north-east without trouble, and it seemed just possible that the danger threatening her had gone away. If the U-boat, assuming there was one, had been shadowing the ship during the night, she had not, so far as was known, fired a torpedo. Could it be that she had damaged herself in collision with the ship? There were more questions than answers.

The sun came up on the 20th into a fine, cloudless sky and the wind was blowing force 5 from the east-south-east, with a moderate sea running. It was a typical fresh South Atlantic morning, having all the indications of a warm day to come. Martyn's star sights, taken at dawn, had fixed the ship's position as 290 miles north of Ilha da Trindade, a tiny island, no more than a tall rock, once used as a departure point by sailing ships bound around the Cape of Good Hope for Australia.

At 0650 the *St Usk* was on a course of 038° and making 9 knots when she steamed into the cross wires of *U-161*'s periscope and Albrecht Achilles gave the order to fire. Seconds later Chief Officer Martyn, who was in the port wing of the bridge, felt the ship stagger under him and heard a muffled explosion from aft. He swung around quickly, in time to see a tall column of water and debris erupt from the port side of No.5 hold. This was followed by the heavy wooden main-topmast crashing to the deck, bringing with it a tangled mess of rigging, halyards and aerials. The sudden violent racing of the *St Usk*'s engine, indicating the loss of her propeller, added to the chaos of the moment.

Captain Moss reached the bridge to find his ship in her death throes, the waves already lapping over her after deck as she settled by the stern. By some miracle only one man had been injured by the explosion, a DEMS gunner who was trapped below decks with a sprained ankle and slight head injuries. While efforts were being made to extricate this man, Moss ordered an emergency aerial to be rigged. This was done, but when it came to transmitting an SOS it was found that the delicate valves of the *St Usk*'s main and emergency transmitters had been smashed by the blast. Their voice was silent.

Although the ship had only a slight list to port and her rate of sinking had slowed, Moss assessed the situation to be hopeless and did not hesitate to order his men to abandon ship. Both lifeboats were lowered without difficulty, care being taken to stow the portable lifeboat transmitter in the starboard boat before lowering. As an added precaution, all four liferafts were also launched. Less than fifteen minutes after the torpedo had hit, all hands were in the boats and pulling away from the ship, the after deck of which was now awash to the height of the 4-inch gun platform.

The *St Usk*, having survived the perils of the sea for thirty-four years, did not die easily. It was 0750, an hour after she had been hit, before the old ship finally gave up the fight and slid beneath the waves. Her crew, who were busy transferring the provisions from the surplus liferafts to the boats, broke off and watched in silence as she went. The last tin of rations had been handed across when Martyn, in charge of No.1 lifeboat, saw the submarine come to the surface and head towards them.

The U-boat was big, around 280 feet long and of about 1,200 tons displacement, Martyn estimated. The emblem painted on the fore end of her conning tower appeared to represent a shield bearing a Viking ship, while alongside that was the outline of a submarine cancelled by a white cross, possibly indicating that the U-boat had sunk an Allied submarine. She mounted an 88mm on her forward casing and six Oerlikons around the conning tower.

Figures in uniform appeared in the conning tower and Martyn instinctively shrank back as one of them raised his binoculars to study the boat. After a few minutes the man lowered his glasses and the U-boat moved off towards the other lifeboat, leaving Martyn to heave a sigh of relief. He was not, after all, to be made a prisoner of war.

The U-boat went alongside the other boat and Martyn licked his lips as he watched mugs of coffee being handed to the survivors. He edged his own boat closer, but backed off when he saw the *St Usk*'s second officer, B.J. Derry, being taken aboard the submarine. He was followed by Captain Moss and Third Radio Officer V.J. Mason. Martyn later learned that the two younger officers were taken as a result of Moss, who had prudently removed all signs of his rank, refusing to identify himself as the ship's captain when challenged.

The U-boat commander then signalled Martyn to bring his boat alongside. This he did with extreme reluctance, and his heart sank when, having tied the boat up to the submarine's casing, he too was ordered aboard.

Martyn found Kapitänleutnant Albrecht Achilles to be a neat, courteous man, speaking excellent English with hardly a trace of an accent. He was dressed in tropical rig of khaki jacket and shorts, and his epaulettes of rank were faded through long exposure to the sun and wind. To Martyn's great relief, Achilles made no move to take him prisoner, but struck up a friendly conversation, in the course of which he gave Martyn an approximate position and a course to steer for the nearest Brazilian port, Bahia, some 500 miles to the west. In response to Martyn's request for medical help for the injured DEMS gunner, Achilles sent the U-boat's doctor down to look at the man. He also passed down three tins of drinking water.

Encouraged by the helpful attitude of the submarine commander, Martyn questioned Achilles about the mysterious bumps felt aboard the *St Usk* on the night of the 19th. Achilles denied being in collision with the ship, but did admit to firing two torpedoes at her that night, one of which had missed astern and the other passing ahead of the ship. Martyn was left with the impression that Achilles had fired rather more than two torpedoes, but was reluctant to admit to this. As to the mystery of the bumps in the night, Martyn concluded that they might have been the result of *U-161*'s torpedoes striking the ship and failing to explode.

While Martyn and Achilles were in conversation, one of the U-boat's crew jumped into the lifeboat and commandeered the portable transmitter. Martyn protested loudly, but Achilles, while expressing regret, pointed out that he could not afford to have his position given away. There was no denying the sense of this and Martyn, mindful of the kindness already shown by Achilles, made no further protest.

As there now seemed no point in delaying the inevitable, Martyn made ready to return to his boat. Before leaving, he shook hands with Captain Moss and his two fellow prisoners, offering to take messages home for them, assuming the boats reached the land. This prompted Moss to reveal his identity to Achilles and asked him to release Derry and Mason. Having achieved his object, Achilles agreed and the young officers, looking vastly relieved, rejoined the others in the boats. Before being taken down the conning tower hatch, Moss wrote a short note to his wife and handed it to Martyn. With genuine regret, Martyn shook his captain's hand again and jumped down into the boat. *U-161*'s diesels then roared into life and she moved off, heading in a southerly direction.

At 1045 the two lifeboats hoisted their sails and set off in company, running before the fresh east-south-easterly breeze.

160

The boats were not overcrowded, Martyn's boat carrying twenty men, while the other boat, in charge of Second Officer Derry, had twenty-seven. During the night the boats lost contact with each other and by daylight on the 21st Martyn found that his boat was alone. Assuming the other boat, which was carrying more weight, must have dropped astern, he lowered his sails and waited. After drifting for some hours with no sight of Derry, Martyn decided to press on for the land.

For the first five days they made good progress, the wind being steady, the weather perfect, with the days not too hot and the nights pleasantly cool. An awning, made up of the boat cover and canvas screens taken from the rafts, was rigged and, with an ample supply of food and water, the survivors were as comfortable as could be expected under the circumstances.

At 0800 on Sunday 26 September, after sailing steadily westwards for six days, a high-flying aircraft was sighted. Smoke floats were set off, but achieved no result, the plane passing overhead apparently without seeing them. But hope returned in the early afternoon, when another aircraft came in flying low. The plane began to circle the lifeboat and they knew they had been seen. The aircraft, a United States patrol plane, dropped tins of food and a message advising the survivors that a ship was coming to their rescue, adding the welcome news that the *St Usk*'s other lifeboat had already been picked up. Before flying off the American pilot gave Martyn a position. The boat was only 130 miles to the south-east of Bahia.

It all seemed cut and dried. After six days of not unduly arduous sailing, rescue was at hand. But then things began to go wrong. For the next twenty-six hours the men searched the horizon in vain. Not a wisp of smoke nor a mast-top was sighted. Then, just after four o'clock on the afternoon of the 27th, when all hope of early rescue was fading, an aircraft with Brazilian markings appeared and twice circled the boat before flying off to the south. Apart from a wave of the hand from the pilot, there was no communication, but Martyn was confident that help was at hand. Again he was disappointed.

Night came and with it deteriorating weather, the wind rising to gale force and heaping up a dangerous sea. This continued for the following twenty-four hours and, although those on board were wet and miserable, the boat sailed well before the wind. By daybreak on the 29th the weather was easing and full daylight revealed low-lying land ahead.

Martyn had no real idea of his position and turned the boat to sail parallel to the coast, looking for signs of civilization. Some hours later a lighthouse and a few isolated houses were sighted. At the same time a small ship was seen, but although smoke floats were burned and rockets fired, the ship passed by. Being by now hardened to disappointment, Martyn decided to close the coast and attempt to land. As he altered course for the lighthouse, the ship suddenly turned about and steamed towards them.

Their rescuer was the Brazilian ship *Porta Segua*, which towed the lifeboat into an anchorage close under the lighthouse. This they discovered was at Morro Sao Paulo, some 30 miles south of Bahia. The survivors spent the night on board the *Porta Segua*, the Master of which obliged Martyn by sending a cable to the British Consul at Bahia. Next afternoon the survivors reboarded their lifeboat and were towed to Bahia by a local schooner.

At 1300 on the 30th, after having sailed a distance of 750 miles in nine days twelve hours, Martyn and his nineteen companions stepped ashore on Brazilian soil. They later heard that the rest of their crewmates, Second Officer Derry and twenty-six men, had been picked up by the Spanish ship *Al Bareda* on the 25th, and landed at Rio de Janeiro, from whence the *St Usk* had set sail ten days earlier.

U-161 claimed only one more victim after the *St Usk*, sinking on 26 September the 4998-ton Brazilian steamer *Itapage*. Twenty-four hours later, and only 100 miles to the north of the spot where Martyn's lifeboat was then being circled by the Brazilian patrol plane, *U-161* was herself sunk by a US Navy Catalina. Achilles and Moss, captor and captive, found a common grave in the depths of the South Atlantic.

22

Two of a Kind

During the course of a voyage, be it long or short, the British merchant seaman inevitably becomes deeply attached to his ship, no matter how old and ugly she may be, for she is both his livelihood and his temporary home. Not surprisingly, when someone tries to take her from him he will fight back.

Throughout the long war at sea it was only on rare occasions that the British merchant ship was able to make use of her limited armament against a visible enemy. All too often the attack took place in the dead of night and the crash of the torpedo, quickly followed by the sea flooding into the ship, was the first and only indication of danger. Usually it was then too late for anything but the undignified scramble for the boats and rafts. However, when given the opportunity to take up arms in their defence, the merchant seamen did so with a remarkable efficiency born out of desperation and anger.

The 4212-ton steamship *Newton Pine*, owned by the Graig Shipping Company, left Buenos Aires on 27 November 1940 bound for Freetown. She was loaded with 1,134 tons of wheat and barley consigned to a British port as yet unnamed. Built in 1925, the *Newton Pine* carried a crew of thirty-seven and was armed with a 12-pounder and a 4-inch, both sad reminders of another war fought twenty-two years earlier. In command was Captain C.N. Woolner, a master mariner not to be trifled with, as indeed were most of his breed.

On the passage north to Freetown the ship sailed unescorted, following the recommended Admiralty route given to Woolner by the British Consul in Buenos Aires. As she steamed across the broad, unruffled acres of the South Atlantic, the war seemed like a fading nightmare, yet far to the north, unknown to Woolner, Convoy HX 90 was making its way slowly eastwards through foul weather and into the U-boat trap that would all but destroy it.

Captain Woolner was also unaware that, after savaging Convoy HX 84 in early November, the pocket-battleship *Admiral Scheer* had moved southwards, sinking the British ship *Port Hobart* off Bermuda on the 24th of the month. But even if he had known of these events taking place in the north, this would not have affected Woolner's determination to press on. He had an ocean to cross, a cargo to deliver. However, he was not naive enough to drop his guard altogether. The guns were exercised at every possible opportunity on the passage.

The Equator was crossed in the early hours of the morning of 13 December and by noon that day the *Newton Pine* was only three days steaming from Freetown. The weather was perfect, with a light easterly wind and the sea disturbed only by the ship's wake as she zig-zagged her way to the north-east. At ten minutes before four that afternoon the *Newton Pine*'s second officer, nearing the end of his four-hour watch on the bridge, saw a torpedo break the surface at about 1,500 yards off the starboard quarter. Acting instinctively, he ordered the helm hard to port, swinging the ship away from the track of the torpedo. Pausing only to throw the switch of the alarm bells, he ran back out to the starboard wing of the bridge and had the hair-raising experience of seeing the torpedo, clearly visible just below the surface, pass along the ship's side no more than 15 feet from her hull plates.

Called to the bridge, Captain Woolner was witness to the unfulfilled torpedo porpoising across the bows, just 1,500 yards ahead of the ship. Quickly, he brought the *Newton Pine* around on to a course of 315°, putting her, as far as he could judge, stern-on to the hidden submarine.

Half an hour later, when Woolner and his chief officer were in the chartroom composing a radio message to be sent to warn all ships that a U-boat was about, the two men heard the sound of gunfire. They rushed out into the wing of the bridge to see shells bursting in the water astern of the ship. Their attacker was a surfaced submarine some 4 or 5 miles off on the port quarter.

Altering course to put the submarine directly astern, so presenting the smallest possible target, Woolner ordered the 4-inch gun, already manned, to open fire. The battle for survival was on.

Keeping the submarine astern, Woolner directed the fire of the 4-inch from the bridge. The *Newton Pine*'s first shell fell short and to the left, her second in line with the submarine, but still short. Woolner increased the range and deflection, and the third shot landed very close to the enemy.

The *Newton Pine* was by this time steaming at her absolute maximum speed of 9 knots, with the submarine's shells falling anything up to 100 yards short of her rounded stern. It soon became evident, however, that the submarine was rapidly over-taking the ship and, as the distance shortened, so the spouts of water sent up by the exploding shells crept nearer, until they were only 50 yards astern and then straddling the her.

It now became clear to those on the bridge of the *Newton Pine* that the enemy was attacking with two guns, both of which were mounted immediately forward of her conning tower. She flew no ensign and carried no identifying marks, but the shape of her conning tower, unusually long and square-cut at the fore end, led Woolner to believe she must be Italian.

The *Newton Pine*'s after gun's crew were now well in their stride, firing as fast as they could load and putting to good effect the lessons learned in the regular gun drills on the passage north. Their shells were now falling close to and directly ahead of the pursuing submarine, which was at times disappearing from sight behind the fountain's of water sent up by the exploding shells.

Woolner, his knuckles showing white as he gripped the after rail of the bridge, knew it must be only a matter of time before his ship was overcome by the superior fire-power of the enemy. When a shell exploded only 10 feet off the ship's side abreast the after hold he decided that drastic evasive action was called for. Ordering the 4-inch to cease fire, he put the helm hard to star-board and swung the ship's head through 60 degrees, putting the enemy on the starboard quarter. This was a risky move, but

Woolner hoped it might confuse the submarine's gunners and also give his own gun's crew a clearer view of their target.

The ploy worked, the enemy submarine's shells beginning to overshoot the *Newton Pine*, landing between 50 and 150 yards off her port bow. Woolner now ordered the 4-inch to re-commence firing and to his great satisfaction the first shell from the gun scored a hit on the submarine's waterline, sending up a cloud of smoke and spray. The second shell exploded immediately in front of her conning tower. The submarine ceased firing and rolled heavily to one side, almost submerging her conning tower. She then straightened up with only the upper part of her conning tower above the water. A few seconds later she was gone from sight. The *Newton Pine*'s masthead lookout reported seeing her half-surface two or three times before she finally disappeared.

Woolner, uncertain whether his adversary had sunk or merely submerged to make a torpedo attack, ordered a smoke float to be dropped astern. When the black, oily smoke had formed a thick screen between the ship and the enemy's last known position, he steamed off to the north-west at full speed. A good lookout was kept for the submarine during the rest of daylight and throughout the following night, but she did not reappear.

Altogether, the gun fight had lasted no more than half an hour, during which time the *Newton Pine*'s 4-inch fired twenty-two rounds and, in Woolner's estimation, the submarine had replied with fifty or sixty shells. The merchant ship had suffered no damage or casualties, although there had been a near-disaster in her galley. In the excitement of the action the ship's cook, who had taken it on himself to carry buckets of hot tea to the thirsty 4-inch crew, unfortunately completely forgot that he had a batch of bread in the oven. Only the timely disappearance of the enemy saved the loaves from burning and the cook from the wrath of Captain Woolner.

The identity and ultimate fate of the *Newton Pine*'s attacker never came to light, but it seems possible she may have been the Italian submarine *Foca*, which was reported missing in the Mediterranean on an unspecified day in December 1940. It may well be that the *Foca* ventured out into the Atlantic, and met her end at the hands of Captain Woolner's gunners.

The gallant *Newton Pine* survived another two years of the war. Then, on 15 October 1942, when in a convoy bound west across the Atlantic, she lost contact with the other ships in a storm and was never seen again. It was claimed, but never confirmed, that she was sunk on 16 October in position 55° N 30° W by *U-704*.

Coincidental with the *Newton Pine*'s gun duel with her unidentified adversary, another British ship, the *Sarastone*, was riding out a howling gale in the Western Approaches. She was at the same time attempting to keep station in Convoy OG 47, bound from Milford Haven to Gibraltar. God and the weather were not on her side.

Built in 1929, and owned by Stone & Rolfe, the 2473-ton *Sarastone* was a typical collier of her day. Small, sturdy and, like all overworked, ageing ships, she was subject to frequent recurring bouts of engine trouble. However, to Captain John Herbert and his crew of twenty-two the recalcitrant engine was a fact of life to be taken in their stride. There were worse things to worry about in the war.

When the *Sarastone* left Barry on 7 December 1940 she was loaded with 4,060 tons of coal, right down to her marks, and with precious little freeboard to keep at bay the North Atlantic in the depths of winter. In times of peace she would have limped down the Bristol Channel at her own pace and, with the exception of the unavoidable exposed crossing of the Bay of Biscay, prudently hugged the coast for much of the 1,100-mile passage to Gibraltar. Unfortunately, on this occasion she was under orders to join a convoy at Milford Haven.

Having the protection of the convoy around him was of some comfort to Captain Herbert, for the enemy's war against British shipping was at its height and the *Sarastone*, slow as a plodding carthorse, was armed only with a 12-pounder and two light machine guns. But it was the route the convoy was to follow that caused Herbert most concern. The southern exit from the Bristol Channel was now securely sealed off by British minefields and OG 47 was to proceed around the north of Ireland and then steam 200 miles out into the Atlantic before heading south. The *Sarastone* would therefore be venturing out into deep, unfamiliar waters, and for much of the time would be far from a port of refuge should she get into difficulties.

John Herbert's worst fears were realized in the early hours of 20 December when the *Sarastone* was 240 miles west of Cape Finisterre and labouring in the grip of a full gale. Out of the blue the engine-room reported a serious defect in the port boiler, which would have to be shut down, leaving the ship with only half power, which in the *Sarastone* was the next best thing to heaving to. Herbert informed the Convoy Commodore of his predicament and was told to proceed independently, keeping a rendezvous with the convoy, if able, at noon on the 22nd. Five hours later the *Sarastone*, making only 2 knots in the heavy seas, had dropped astern and out of sight of the other ships. The heavily loaded collier, shipping green seas at every roll and barely maintaining steerage way, was left to fight her battles alone.

Strenuous efforts were made to repair the *Sarastone*'s leaking boiler, but without proper equipment her engineers could do little. Fortunately, the weather moderated over the next twenty-four hours, but by then the overstrained starboard boiler was also beginning to give trouble. Herbert decided to make for the nearest port, Lisbon, while he still had power left. Ignoring the proposed rendezvous with the convoy, he hauled over to the east, determined to close the Portuguese coast as soon as possible.

Soon after she settled down on her new course the *Sarastone*'s wireless operator intercepted a message from the Admiralty warning of an enemy submarine sighted to the south of the ship and near the rendezvous point. The submarine in question was, in fact, shadowing Convoy OG 47 and would attack it later that day.

The improvement in the weather continued and the 22nd dawned fine, with a light north-westerly breeze, slight sea and the horizon sharp and clear. Nursing her one remaining boiler, the *Sarastone* was averaging 5½ knots and seemed sure of reaching Lisbon on the night of the 24th. The ill wind that had forced the ship to leave the convoy now blew fair for John Herbert and his crew. Christmas spent in a neutral Portuguese port was a bonus they had not anticipated.

The first sign of trouble came near the end of the afternoon watch when the Second Officer sighted what he thought to be a fishing boat about 4 miles off the starboard beam. Being a cautious man, he called the Captain to the bridge. Herbert, squinting into the sun, then low down on the horizon, could not recognize the silhouette of the vessel, but his suspicions were aroused. The *Sarastone* was then some 300 miles from the nearest land and in 600 fathoms of water, a most unlikely spot in which to encounter fishermen. As a first precaution, he ordered all hands on deck. A few minutes later the object moved out of the direct line of the sun and Herbert found himself focusing his binoculars on a submarine heading for his ship at speed.

The Italian submarine *Moncenigo*'s attack on Convoy OG 47 on the 21st had been something of a disappointment for her commander, Capitano di Corvetta Alberto Agostini. He had succeeded in sinking only the small Swedish steamer *Mangen*, before being chased off by the convoy escorts. Now he was on the lookout for easier prey – and he appeared to have found it.

Captain Herbert, still not certain that he was facing the enemy, took the only sensible action open to him. He put the *Sarastone* stern-on to the approaching submarine, ordered his gun's crew to close up on the 12-pounder, which was mounted on the collier's poop, and waited for developments.

He did not have long to wait. The *Moncenigo*'s first shell, fired as the *Sarastone* was still swinging to her helm, fell short, as did her subsequent shots. The range was still too great for the 12-pounder and Herbert passed the word aft for the gunlayer to hold his fire until the submarine was within 2000 yards. When the range was closed the *Sarastone*'s gun barked and the fight was on.

Although the enemy submarine appeared to be using only one of her two deck guns and the rate of fire was slow, shells began to land uncomfortably close to the British ship as she ran away

169

at full speed. Herbert concentrated on keeping his stern to the enemy and braced himself for the battering his ship must inevitably take. Then the impossible happened. The *Sarastone*'s 12-pounder, carefully laid by her gunlayer James O'Neil, scored a direct hit on the *Moncenigo*. Flames and smoke shot into the air, the submarine slewed round until she was beam-on and, to the accompaniment of cheers from the collier's crew, a second shell slammed home.

The submarine began to submerge and Herbert, his ire thoroughly aroused, ordered the bridge machine guns to open fire on the enemy. The range was too long for the light Hotchkiss guns, but the 12-pounder continued to lob shells close to the submarine, whose efforts to submerge seemed to be unsuccessful.

The *Sarastone* was now drawing away and when the range increased to 4000 yards Herbert ordered the 12-pounder to cease fire. The submarine was still on the surface and apparently stopped, with yellow smoke pouring from her after end. She was a sitting target but with only seven shells left in the 12-pounder magazine, Herbert resisted the impulse to close the enemy and finish her off. At 1650, with the submarine out of sight, he stood down his gun's crews and resumed course for Lisbon.

The Portuguese capital was reached on the night of the 24th and Captain John Herbert and his men were able to spend a well-deserved Christmas in port. Repairs were carried out to the *Sarastone*'s boilers, and she was eventually able to continue her voyage. In Gibraltar she received twenty-three shells to replace those she had used in the fight with the *Moncenigo*, but such was the state of British ammunition stocks overseas at this stage of the war that no cordite charges could be supplied for the shells. It was indeed fortunate for the *Sarastone* that she did not fall in with the enemy again on her homeward passage.

The *Moncenigo* did not sink, but she was forced to retire to lick her wounds for a very long time. She was next heard of, under a new commander, in the Mediterranean in March 1942. Her continuing career, however, was as undistinguished as before. She accounted for only one Allied ship, the 1500-ton

French-flag *Sainte Marcelle*, before being despatched by US aircraft in a raid on Cagliari on 13 May 1943.

The plucky little *Sarastone*'s luck had run out eighteen months earlier. She was bombed and sunk when leaving the Spanish port of Huelva on 29 October 1941.

23

Requiem

The memories of the Second World War are now more than half a century old and fading fast, but it will not go amiss to recall again the terrible losses Britain's Merchant Navy suffered in those dark days. In August 1945, when the conflict which had spread to the furthest reaches of the oceans at last drew to a close, the final reckoning was 2,426 British merchant ships of 11,331,933 tons sunk and 29,180 seamen lost. For almost three years the outcome of the struggle had hung in the balance, needing only the merest wavering to tip the scales the wrong way. Between May 1940 and July 1941 sinkings were averaging sixty-six ocean-going ships a month, the climax being reached in May 1941, with twenty ships lost for every week that passed. It would then have been easy for Britain's merchant seamen, poorly paid and casually employed, to have adopted the attitude of many dockers, miners and shipyard workers who, conscious of their indispensability, regularly held their country to ransom using the fashionable weapon of industrial action. If the merchant seamen, who were strictly speaking civilians, had refused to sail the ships – and the temptation to do just that must have been very great at times – then Britain would have gone under, for no nation can fight for long with stomachs empty and arsenals unstocked.

But despite the torpedoes, the shells, the mines, the bombs and the one-in-three prospect of a cold, unmarked grave, Britain's merchant seamen never once refused to leave port. It is sad to reflect that the bravery of these men went almost unnoticed when the accolades were handed out. For the 29,180 who died, most of them denied even the dignity of a few yards of duck canvas, there remains only a forgotten memorial in an obscure corner of London's Tower Hill. That the men who died should not be remembered, except by those they left behind, is perhaps only another demonstration of human frailty. That the *raison d'être* of the sacrifice they made should be ignored is incomprehensible.

The British Commonwealth of Nations, as the Empire of yesteryear is now called, once reached out to the four corners of the globe, covering over 13 million square miles, with a population of 450 million. Britain herself, with a large population and an economy based on manufacturing industry, was then wholly dependent on her merchant ships, not only for her own sustenance, but for communication and trade with her vast territories overseas. It is then not surprising that, at the beginning of the 20th century, the Red Ensign flew over almost 50 per cent of the world's commercial shipping. In fact, such was the dominance of British ships that they carried over half the world's maritime trade in their bottoms.

The advent of the First World War highlighted the importance of this fleet and, sadly, its vulnerability, when submarine warfare was for the first time introduced on a massive and ruthless scale. Britain did not starve, neither did she lack for arms and raw materials, but the price to her Merchant Navy was high, 2,479 ships and 14,879 seamen being lost. The damage was, however, quickly made good, replacement ships being built and crews found to man them. Between the wars, in spite of the catastrophic depression of the early 1930s, British shipping, although never to achieve its dominance of the early days, held firm and in 1939 was once again in a strong position to face up to a prolonged blockade. The necessity for a large British merchant fleet had been revealed for a second time.

The proving of the theory twice in the space of thirty years should have been a salutary lesson to the British people. This was apparently not so, or if the lesson was learnt it was not absorbed. When the Falklands mini-war came along Britain's merchant fleet, for the first time in its long history, was found wanting. Committed at short notice to forming a retaliatory task force,

173

the British government suffered the gross humiliation of having to charter in foreign merchant ships to make up the small 49-ship support fleet. The same thing was repeated in the more recent Gulf War. How was it that a nation which had fought and won the Battle of the Atlantic, sustaining at its height losses of sixty to seventy ships a month, had descended to such impotency?

Much of Britain's merchant tonnage lost in the Second World War was quickly replaced by ships mass-produced in the ship-yards of the United States and Canada. These were all-welded ships of a very basic design, built primarily to see out the duration of the war and, perhaps, a year or two into the peace. Some did not even survive their first crossing of the Atlantic many were sunk before the end of the war. By 1945 the Merchant Navy was many millions of tons down on its pre-war strength. Some of the smaller shipping companies had been all but wiped out and the larger concerns were sadly depleted.

With the peace came the boom and, although Britain was near to economic bankruptcy and on the brink of losing her Empire, there was a rich harvest to be reaped in the maritime fields. The war-ravaged countries of Europe and the Far East were in desperate need of the goods and machinery to rebuild their shattered cities and industries. Within a few years there was a worldwide shortage of shipping and British shipowners, ever with an eye to potential business, began to replenish their fleets.

By 1950, Britain owned nearly 25 per cent of the world's merchant shipping and looked set to regain her pre-eminence of the beginning of the century, when the Red Ensign dominated the trade routes and ports of the world. Over the next twenty-five years, while the uneasy peace of the nuclear deterrent reigned, the steady expansion continued until, in 1975, there were no less than 50 million tons of commercial shipping under the British flag. Then the bubble burst. Today, a quarter of a century on, less than 300 ships sail under the Red Ensign. A mighty fleet that Grand-Admiral Dönitz and all his predatory U-boats failed to destroy has been thrown away, ship by ship, largely through complacency in the face of determined competition from outside.

While the British government is doggedly committed to a policy of free trade, the rest of the world takes a different view. The United States will not allow foreign ships into its coastal trade, nor will most of the mainland European countries. The old Soviet Union still operates a huge fleet, state-owned and subsidised, and moves virtually all its own cargo, coastal and deep-sea. On the Indian sub-continent, in Asia and Africa political pressure is used to secure national cargoes for national-flag ships. And all the while Britain, for centuries the dominant sea power of the world, stubbornly refuses to offer any form of economic or political protection to its ever-dwindling merchant fleet.

Subsidization and protectionism apart, by far the greatest threat to British commercial shipping is the flag of convenience: the safe haven for the unscrupulous shipowner looking for a quick return on his money, with no tax to be paid, no allegiance to be owed and precious few rules to adhere to. Year after year casualty figures prove the majority of flag of convenience ships are poorly manned, equipped and maintained. Yet they continue to operate, apparently free from interference by the august bodies that supposedly police the world's commercial shipping. As a direct result of the low freights they are able to offer, these same ships rarely lack cargoes and are often to be seen plying the seas loaded well below their deliberately rust-streaked Plimsoll marks. Incredible though it may seem, these latter-day free-booters are, in most cases, able to obtain, without difficulty, full insurance cover for their ships and cargoes.

Over the years the situation became so grave that British shipowners having cargo to move found it cheaper to charter in foreign tonnage, thereby condemning their own ships to the slow death of the lay-by berth. The inevitable happened; British ships, made redundant through high running costs, were sold to eagerly awaiting foreign buyers as going concerns. Within a very short space of time these ships were back at sea, under a new flag, often in the same trade, lifting the same cargoes and in direct competition with their previous British owners. Operated on the cheap and with little thought for safety, their profitability was assured. Meanwhile, the British shipowner was forced to turn

175

his shareholders' money to better uses. One by one British shipping companies, some of them household names in the maritime world for hundreds of years, were forced to shut up shop for ever. Today two-thirds of Britain's considerable maritime trade is carried in foreign bottoms, usually flag of convenience.

A succession of British governments, for reasons of dogma or political necessity, has been prepared to pour money into the bottomless coffers of inefficient, overmanned and uneconomical industries ashore. It seems that no price has been too high in order to gain some political advantage. Yet, even in the light of the Falklands and the Gulf War, there has still been no move to offer succour to a dying British Merchant Navy. Britain is now the only western maritime nation totally without governmental support, in cash or in kind, for its merchant shipping. Should she ever become engaged in a major war again, her umbilical cord to the warehouses of the outside world would be slashed through in the opening weeks of the conflict, leaving her people faced with the choice of abject surrender or a slow death in isolation.

Bibliography

Beaver, Paul, *U-boats in the Atlantic*, Patrick Stephens, 1979

Brown, Anthony Cave, *Bodyguard of Lies*, W.H. Allen, 1976

Bucheim, Lothar-Günther, *U-boat War*, Collins, 1978

Churchill, W.S., *The Second World War*, Cassell, 1948

Costello & Hughes, *The Battle of the Atlantic*, Collins, 1977

HMSO, *British Vessels Lost at Sea 1939–45*, Patrick Stephens, 1984

HMSO, *Merchantmen at War*, HMSO, 1944

Hocking, Charles, *Dictionary of Disasters at Sea During the Age of Steam*, Lloyd's Register of Shipping, 1969

Jones, Geoffrey, *Defeat of the Wolf Packs*, William Kimber, 1986

Rohwer, Jürgen, *Axis Submarine Successes 1939–1945*, Patrick Stephens, 1983

Robertson, Terence, *The Golden Horseshoe*, Evans Bros., 1955

Roskill, Captain S.W., *The War at Sea*, HMSO, 1954

Slader, John, *The Fourth Service*, Robert Hale, 1994

Terraine, John, *Business in Great Waters*, Leo Cooper, 1989

Thomas, David A., *The Atlantic Star*, W.H. Allen, 1990

Woon, Basil, *Atlantic Front*, Peter Davies, 1941

The author also wishes to acknowledge the help of the Public Record Office, the Imperial War Museum and the National Maritime Museum.

Index

178

180